TOUGH TACTICS
FOR TOUGH TIMES

TOUGH TACTICS FOR TOUGH TIMES

HOW TO MAINTAIN BUSINESS SUCCESS IN DIFFICULT ECONOMIC CONDITIONS

PATRICK FORSYTH & FRANCES KAY

London and Philadelphia

Publisher's note

Every possible effort has been made to ensure that the information contained in this book is accurate at the time of going to press, and the publishers and authors cannot accept responsibility for any errors or omissions, however caused. No responsibility for loss or damage occasioned to any person acting, or refraining from action, as a result of the material in this publication can be accepted by the editor, the publisher or any of the authors.

First published in Great Britain and the United States in 2009 by Kogan Page Limited

120 Pentonville Road
London N1 9JN
United Kingdom
www.koganpage.com

525 South 4th Street, #241
Philadelphia PA 19147
USA

© Patrick Forsyth and Frances Kay, 2009

ISBN 978 0 7494 5521 7

British Library Cataloguing-in-Publication Data

A CIP record for this book is available from the British Library.

Library of Congress Cataloging-in-Publication Data

Forsyth, Patrick.
    Tough tactics for tough times : how to maintain business success in difficult economic conditions / Patrick Forsyth and Frances Kay.
        p. cm.
    ISBN 978-0-7494-5521-7
    1. Success in business. 2. Business planning. 3. Managerial economics. I. Kay, Frances, 1949- II. Title.
    HF5386.F455 2009
    658.4'09--dc22
                                2008048834

Typeset by Saxon Graphics Ltd, Derby
Printed and bound in Great Britain by MPG Books Ltd, Bodmin, Cornwall

Contents

Introduction – time to keep your nerve

'Things are going to get a lot worse before they get worse.'

Lily Tomlin

If the above quotation is not to prove true, the firm response to deteriorating economic conditions and falling markets, profits and spirits should surely be to take stock – and then take action.

The worst possible reaction is one of shell shock: wishing that conditions will change, that difficulties will go away and believing that there is nothing to do but wait. Most often 'waiting for things to get back to normal' is simply not an option. Things change; and they certainly change – sometimes radically and quickly – when tough economic conditions strike.

Economic and market conditions are said sometimes to go in cycles; but they are ever volatile. The exact definition of 'recession' matters little, and is ignored here; what matters is that when adverse circumstances affect a business the business and its managers respond. This may be in a contained area, as when difficult times hit one particular industry or sector, or perhaps in one geographic area. Or it may be more widespread, as now, when a whole economy seems to wobble.

For instance in marketing, the overall process that brings in the business, a continuing focus on, and commitment to, marketing action is necessary at a time when the gut reaction (in this and many other fields) is to cut indiscriminately at the first sign of trouble. Sales down? Cut advertising and promotion, cut the staff and the training budget and then what... hope that the business will continue unaffected?

A number of factors seem to us to be fundamental: action and attitudes designed to make it more likely that existing customers will be held, new ones still won, the organization kept on track and profitability protected and ideally maintained. Certainly recession affects everyone. Customer attitudes change, their loyalty (even those at a high level at the time) declines. Promotional and sales activity thus need to be organized to bridge that gap and to continue to maximize its effectiveness. In part such thing should be seen not as emergency action, rather as routine, everyday approaches.

What to do and how to do it

Marketing is only one area and there are ideas here for organization, human resources, finance and linked to personal productivity. Stick with marketing for the moment. In competitive times, as now and for the foreseeable future, a number of things are needed – for example:

- *A systematic approach to marketing:* increasing complexity has since made this even more essential; only a well-planned mix is likely to do the right job.
- *Spending enough time:* the time marketing takes, certainly to undertake it well, is often seriously underestimated, especially in the small business. Just putting in the time remains the first step to making the activity work.

- *A customer focus:* this is an ongoing necessity and customers are even more demanding now than the last time similar sorts of economic difficulty threatened; everything needs to be done with an eye on the ways customers want it or find it acceptable.
- *Continuity of action:* marketing was, and remains, an ongoing process needing regular attention; making it fit with the possible feast and famine of a volatile business is one of the challenges.
- *Clear account responsibility:* a dedicated someone definitively in charge of every major customer; in difficult times this becomes even more important.
- *Bullish pricing:* in a recession even a hint from a customer that prices are too high has often tended to lead to instant, and ill-considered, discounting. Price is now better understood for its role as part of the marketing mix, not least as a sign of quality, and organizations are now more likely to set profitable prices with confidence, justifying them rather than trembling if they are challenged
- *Professional selling:* selling is a final link with customers. It can be taken for granted in buoyant times, and must be deployed in the best possible way in any other.

Similarly, promotional activity must create real interest, enquiry handling must confirm efficiency and sales meetings, written proposals and presentations – whatever is necessary in particular businesses –must build interest into confirmation of orders. Furthermore, as one author's (PF) sales manager wisely said long ago, remember that it's not an order until the money is in the bank. Other prudent action will reduce costs, affect staff and operational procedures; indeed every aspect of an organization's operation may need some attention and this applies to organizations of every size.

So what do you do and how can this book help?

Let's be honest, it does not provide a magic formula; you cannot hope to wave it at the approaching thunder-clouds and see them evaporate before your eyes. But, whatever responsibility you have – for a whole organization or a part of it – it can help. Everything mentioned here is a tried and tested idea that can contribute something to you and your business surviving – and perhaps thriving – despite the difficulties. The combined effect of numbers of initiatives can be substantial; for some action – the right action – can make the difference between survival and collapse. So, if there is no magic formula, and there isn't, then progress becomes a question of leaving no stone unturned; anything and everything that might help to some degree must be utilized to catch its positive effect.

Ideas and action

There are ideas here to:

- save money;
- keep orders coming in;
- enable necessary action to be taken promptly and with certainty;
- maintain personal productivity and a focus on important issues and reduce stress.

Amongst the fifty ideas reviewed here are ideas that should work for anyone, others that will suit some and still more that may need some adaptation in order to work for you. Many describe areas where, faced with difficulty, a typical action is to do nothing, at least for a while, by which time the action necessary may be different, more difficult, or more expensive or time consuming to take – all at a time when you want to have time to focus on the priorities.

The fifty-two chapters of the book are varied in length. Some include a brief how-to guide to techniques referred to: see, for example, negotiation on page 49. Others may link directly to action or some further checking may be useful before you apply them. They are presented in random order and relate to a variety of different aspects of a business. This is so that you can dip in and out, skip anything that is (really) not right for you and use this process as part of the taking stock that will lead you to action and changes, changes that may make your survival in reasonable shape possible, indeed likely. We intend also that this review will act as a catalyst, leading directly to discussions and review meetings in the organizations of those who read the book, and that those in turn will take you forward. Most ideas are not solely relevant to commercial organizations, but will make sense for any organization that finds itself with its back to the wall in some way.

Remember that waiting, however hopefully, does not really qualify as considered action and also that while good luck may explain the success of your competitors, it is not to be relied on as a tangible tactic. Tough measures may well be necessary and the sooner you start on them the better.

In Chinese writing the word 'crisis' is expressed in the form, not of one, but of the two Chinese characters shown below.

The first represents the word for 'chaos'. The second signifies the word 'opportunity'.

Interesting, especially considering the age of the Chinese language – and not a bad way to think about, and perhaps respond to, a crisis!

That said, finally, let us make clear that the overall tone here is not doom and gloom. We take the view that you can make a difference. Some of the ideas here have negative connotations and need a certain amount of decisiveness to enact, perhaps even ruthlessness, but the overall outcome that everything aims for is a positive one.

Your attitude throughout the piece

Let's start with a short comment, but one that should pervade your whole attitude and actions taken in response to any kind of difficulty. We'll start by resorting to fiction. The late Douglas Adams made a simple phrase all his own. On the cover of his book *The Hitchhiker's Guide to the Galaxy*, in large, friendly letters, was the message:

Don't Panic!

It is good advice. Action taken in a panic – a well-known phrase makes the point: a blind panic – is rarely going to result in your giving something your best shot.

Action

The only specific action here is an internal, introspective one. Take a deep breath (a metaphorical one if you like), pause and think. What you are seeking, and what this book aims to help you find, are considered responses; balanced ones, too – you don't want to throw the baby out with the bath water or find some short-term 'remedy' that makes more, perhaps worse, problems in the long term.

There may well be a degree of urgency about taking action, but that does not make it sensible to ditch thought and charge at things full tilt.

Given that difficult conditions can sometimes last a while, this may most likely be a danger in the early stages, but it may prove useful to continue to say 'Don't panic' to yourself on a regular basis.

And another idea...

You may want to define the word 'think' as it is used above. You may well need to research, consult, debate, brainstorm and more to produce the considered ideas necessary and ensure their implementation. If doing this involves more than just you to make it happen, so be it.

2

Making decisions – ready, aim… fire

Making decisions can be difficult. Not making them, or making the wrong one, can be disastrous. And making the wrong ones in difficult times can lead from bad to worse.

The assistant looks at the customer, decides they warrant no special attention, and effectively bundles them out of the shop. Later they arrive back, weighed down with expensive purchases, and show just how wrong the assistant's decision was. Big mistake. Remember this scene from the movie *Pretty Woman*? The principle applies to us all. We want to make good decisions and, if we do not, the results may return to haunt us.

It is not easy. Time pressure and lack of information can lead to rushed or ad hoc decisions that cause real problems. For example, in one company someone decided to replace the ageing fleet of delivery vans. Fine, but many customers ordered by the van-full, so similar sized orders no longer exactly fitted a van. Deliveries appeared short and complaints followed. Sales, dispatch, customer service, accounts – all were left with problems because one, seemingly sensible, decision was not made with an eye on all the implications.

Knowing it is not easy can make things worse. In tough times 'fire fighting' can predominate and decisions may well be delayed, perhaps because of fear of the consequences of making the wrong one, and lack of any action itself may then cause worse problems. Yet it is a truism that a delayed decision never gets easier as time goes by; rather the reverse is true. Hiring and firing are good examples. Wait, indecisively, and a good candidate takes another offer and is no longer available. Delay getting rid of someone because of the emotional difficulty and it gets ever harder to bite the bullet.

Action

In tough times you must resolve to make decisions promptly, but do so using a systematic approach: a thorough way of thinking things through, likely to ensure sensible action results. Simple decisions may short-circuit this; but that must be a carefully selected option. The following ten stages will ensure nothing is overlooked.

1. Set objectives: how are you ever going to make a good decision if you are not clear, really clear, what you are aiming at? Objectives should be specific, measurable, achievable, realistic and timed. It is wholly different to decide something because it will 'reduce costs' rather than because it will 'reduce administration costs by 10 per cent during the next three months'.

2. Evaluate objectives: it is important to check broadly – do the objectives conflict in any way with what may be the many and disparate goals of the business? For example, moving slowly on something might save money, but create worse problems.

3. Collect information: ask what information is necessary before a decision can sensibly be taken. For example, deciding on tactical promotional activity may need accurate, up-to-date sales figures.

4. Analyse the information: think it through, do not take it at face value. Sales figures may be down, but why? One large order lost, regular customers varying their timing (so purchasing less one month) could be factors. Investigation should take the lead.

5. Develop alternatives: of all the stages this is the most often overlooked. Many decisions are really 'more of the same, or not', when what is required, especially in difficult times, is some creative thought and some new ideas to consider.

6. Select the 'best' alternative: if you evaluate all the alternatives now on the table (for example, looking at cost, timing, risk, resources and so on), then one must be the 'best' option – even if it is something of a compromise, or a finely balanced choice.

7. Communicate the decision: tell everyone affected, and tell them in an appropriate manner – a brief e-mail, or a meeting to discuss matters? If a decision prompts change, then people involved in implementation must know what is going on, and often must understand and support the change if implementation is to work.

8. Set up any necessary controls: consider and put in place anything that must be checked or measured as action proceeds. So, a decision to change complaint-handling procedures may need to include a measurement of what then happens to customer satisfaction levels.

9. Implement the action: whatever the decision prompts in terms of action must now be carried out, and this means that who will do what and when must be clear.

10. Evaluate the decision: learning from experience is important. If something goes well, you can apply more of the same; if not, in the future you can actively avoid repeating anything that has caused problems.

Good decisions follow sound thinking. Gut-feeling should not be excluded entirely (it often reflects real experience), and should be weighed in the balance. A systematic approach may not guarantee success – but it will make its likelihood greater.

And another idea...

If you are not certain what to do about something, do not just flip a coin – consult. Ask your boss, a colleague or a member of your team what they think – there is no monopoly on good ideas and they might just provide an insight that helps you move on promptly. Even the one-man business can do this through networking (more of that in Chapter 35).

3

Taking time can be the quickest and surest way

A participant came forward after a seminar posing a question. How could something be changed? The details don't matter, but what happened illustrated something important. As the course tutor (PF) thought about it, it seemed to him that there was no instant solution. A campaign of a series of actions, however, seemed likely to make a difference. The questioner looked puzzled as this was described. As the conversation progressed it became clear that they had assumed that there would be one instant solution to the problem. The questioner had clearly not thought about the matter in any other way and, told that a more complex solution was necessary, their first reaction was puzzlement.

This is a symptom of today's 'sound-bite world' perhaps; everything needs to be instant. Sadly life is not like that; many things need to be worked through, and often only a number of different influences can create the required change. Furthermore there is a distinct tendency in tough times for people to seek instant solutions: take some action – sort out one problem – move on to the next matter.

Action

The action starts with a simple resolution. Tough times bring problems. Realistically some of them will not be solved at a stroke; they need thinking through and they need a number of things to be done to create whatever outcome is wanted.

You may need to resist the temptation to rush at things; indeed there is a possibility that this could lead to a worse situation. It is better to take a month, or more, to sort something out and get it right than to aim to fix it in a moment and find the problem simply returns, and worsens.

And another idea...

If time is needed to effect change do make a careful note and monitor the process. For instance, you may want to check progress after a month has passed if you feel something should have reached a certain stage in that time. If progress does not go as expected or planned, some fine-tuning may be necessary, fine-tuning that could see the end result emerge sooner or prevent an over-run getting out of hand. As the section on managing your time makes clear, the more you have to do and the greater the difficulty, the greater the benefit of remaining organized and keeping on top of things.

4

Getting paid

No one needs reminding of the importance of cash flow. In tough times cash needs getting in fast. And make no mistake: the cost of poor cash flow, both in bank charges and more, might frighten many people who have not thought about it for a while. Even in a small organization this is not something to neglect.

The remark quoted in the introduction – the sales manager's comment that it's not an order until the money is in the bank – should give us all pause for thought. It may be a truism, but many businesses are lax – sometimes extraordinarily lax – at getting the money in to a reasonable time scale. In one company, one of us (PF) was once asked, in the context of a business writing course, to critique a series of letters chasing debtors. There were eight different ones, varying in sequence in their degree of strength, but entirely spoiled by the fact that every single one had printed in red type across the top the words 'Final Demand'. Manifestly the majority were not – and that cannot have helped them to get people to take them seriously.

Of one thing you can be sure: those you do business with will very likely be suffering the same difficulties you are, and will be actively delaying payment; certainly payment to those who do not chase.

Action

So, we want to be paid certainly and promptly. This leads to three areas of action:

■ Do not deal with people who cannot pay: credit checks are always a sensible thing to do, more so in difficult times. Do not skimp them and, even more important, do not ignore them. It is easy when every order counts to give someone the benefit of the doubt – you accept the order, knowing that the check is not as good as you would like and 'hope for the best'. Don't do it – it is better not to have the business than to have it (and the attendant costs) and then not get paid.

■ Check your payment terms: these may not have been changed for a long time; sometimes too long. Make sure that they are appropriate, and in particular make sure that any opportunity to vary them on the side of safety and cash flow preservation is taken. For example, does your business lend itself to some payment being made up front (something that might allow you to deal with those with a less than perfect credit rating) and if so do you insist on it, and is it a high enough proportion of the whole? Also do you charge for any necessary extras in the best way? (Look no further than Ryanair if you want to see these opportunities maximized.)

■ Chase the debtors: follow your payment terms, decide how many times you will chase and do so firmly. For instance, you might send a polite reminder, a strong reminder, repeat the reminder with a threat that the next stage becomes legal – then send a solicitor's letter. And never make threats you go back on. If you say something will happen on the 10th then make it happen. Anything else is just an invitation to take longer.

In addition, it may be necessary to talk to your bank about how to improve the management of your cash flow, and to others (for instance, debt collectors) too; if so do it sooner rather than later.

And another idea...

Many debt chasing contacts are made by telephone. Some calls may be more effective when made standing up. Yes, really! Try it. This applies because such calls need a fair bit of assertiveness to be displayed, and this is more easily done standing up. It creates an antidote to the 'Sorry to worry you, but I wonder if perhaps...' approach.

5

Guerrilla tactics that work – competitor analysis

As a general rule, keeping an eye on the opposition is a good way to make sure your organization stays ahead of the game. In tough times, it is essential to spend time studying your competitors. Why? Because, at the very least, it's an information-gathering process about the current state of the market. At best, it is a means of developing a niche area or minimizing the risks that can affect your own organization. Some people argue that it is better to be 'first' than 'best'.

The well-known scenario about the tiger hunters in the jungle puts this important issue in context. There were two hunters and as they were emerging from the trees they suddenly spotted a tiger coming towards them. One of the hunters immediately bent down and started to put on his trainers. 'What on earth are you doing?' asked his companion. 'You'll never outrun that tiger.' 'I don't need to run faster than the tiger,' the first hunter replied. 'All I have to do is to run faster than you.'

It makes sense, doesn't it? In difficult times there's no need to put the competition out of business. Just having an edge over one or two will be enough to enable you to survive. But first of all you need to know who these people are.

Competitors are companies offering similar products or services to you; or companies offering the same products or services. They could be businesses that might offer the same or similar products or services in the future. Alternatively they could be organizations that will remove the need for such products or services as your organization provides. Whoever they are, their objectives are the same as yours – to grow, make money and succeed.

'Never underestimate the enemy.' Wise words, but often ignored. To gain advantage over the competition means knowing how they think, how they might act, what their strengths are, where their weaknesses lie. It also means knowing when and how they are vulnerable, where they can be attacked and knowing when the risk of attack is too great.

Action

1. Work out: Why do you need this information? What do you want to find out? How are you going to do it? Who will analyse the data? How will you use the information once you've collected it? What results do you want to achieve having got it?

2. Find out: Who are your nearest three direct competitors? Who would you regard as indirect competitors? Which of these organizations is growing, static or declining? What can you learn from their operation and advertising? How would you describe their strengths and weaknesses?

   What differentiates your business (products or services) from theirs?

   (Don't forget that in normal economic times markets are constantly changing – legally in relation to regulations and statutes, politically and in terms of technology). In order to survive in tough times, a business owner or operator needs to be able to adapt quickly to suit current trends and reap any possible benefits.

3. Gather information: Carry out your research – look, listen and learn. Visit your competitors' locations to observe how they do business, set out their products, offer their services. How do their staff treat customers?

   One way of doing this is called 'mystery shopping' – market research companies use this method to measure quality of service or gather specific information about products and services. But there's absolutely no reason why you can't do this yourself (unless of course your face is well-known to the opposition). If you delegate the job to a third party, this person must pose as a normal customer purchasing a product, asking questions, registering a complaint or behaving in whatever way you direct. They then report back to you with detailed feedback on what transpired. (Think back to the episode of the TV programme *Fawlty Towers* that featured the hotel inspector.)

   You could ask your own customers their opinion about your competitors. Keep an eye on competitors' marketing and advertising. Who is their target audience and what percentage of market share do they hold? Visit trade shows and exhibitions that they attended. If possible, go along to presentations or speeches given by members of their staff. Observe what appears in print about them – in professional journals, the business press, local newspapers and trade association publications.

4. Process the data: Study and analyse the findings. What should become apparent are trends and patterns. These should be related to your organization's development, profitability and market positioning.

5. Report findings: Set up a system for evaluating the results. Feedback is essential for everyone involved – the information gatherers, the processors and the decision makers. Ask the questions: Was the information useful? Was it understood? How was it interpreted? What was the result of its use? Was it worth it?

And another idea...

Remember, the value of knowledge is difficult to calculate. You can't be sure how or when you are going to use it. But in tough times, you can be sure that ignorance is far more costly. It can result in missed opportunities, or loss of customers. At the worst extreme the business itself could fail as a result of inactivity in certain crucial areas.

Don't lose out – keep your antennae tuned. Competitive intelligence could be your secret weapon in difficult times.

6

Idea generation – thinking laterally

You don't have to be an economist to anticipate when your business is likely to hit a rough patch. When times are difficult, you need to implement smart ideas that will ensure you have a prosperous future. Thinking ahead for the short term makes sense in the current climate because it gives you (and the business) the chance of a less bumpy ride. This means that you need to harness the ability to make the right decisions. And what are they? Ones that will add impetus to your business – quickly and effectively.

If you're not familiar with the process called the 'balanced business scorecard', this is so named because it works on the premise that business strategy and financial considerations should be looked at equally. In tough times this is essential for two reasons. Figures are what measure the temperature of the business. Doing the right things is more important than doing things right. If you give equal consideration to financial projections and strategic thinking, it ensures decisions taken now will encourage further growth and smooth the path immediately ahead.

Take, for example, the fact that most business leaders know where they want to be in four to five years, possibly ten years, time. Applying similar principles, if you want to work out where you'll be in one year's time, you must make the right decisions now in order to get there. If your goals are not clearly defined, you cannot safeguard the future. You can play around with financial figures, projections, and flow charts as much as you like. You can adapt and change as often as you wish, but this won't work. Numbers alone cannot fully represent strategy. Actions alone, however well intentioned, won't help.

When the economic climate is tough no business can afford to spend precious time fire fighting. Instead you should be generating sound ideas. The good news is that the 'balanced business scorecard' process, as defined below, is simple to implement.

Action

Part one

Regard the process like a cascade – asking the following questions:

- Vision: What do you want the organization to be like next year? What is working well at the moment and can be developed?

- Mission: What should employee numbers, turnover, profit, size of key customers, market positioning be by then?

- Strategy: Decide what positioning and competitive strategies are needed to get there – as of now.

- Objectives: What – specifically – needs to be done/changed/reformed?

- Business plan, metrics, action plan, dates: What will the goals, actions, milestones and measures be?

The benefit of this cascade (the generation of effective short-term ideas) is that it works in reverse too. But don't try to do the second part without having done the first part – that won't work!

Part two

Work out the answers to the following:

■   What are the measures you have to achieve?

■   What, in specific terms, must you do to achieve them?

■   How will you set yourself apart from competitors in winning business?

■   What resources will you need to do this? Who will you target, and what skills and standards will you need to apply to get there?

■   What will the organization be like if you achieve all of this?

These questions must be answered fully, with realistic, achievable targets taking into account the current economic climate. Work on the actual situation, and avoid 'what-ifs'.

If you're a business owner or organization director, you must involve your senior management team in order to facilitate this process. They should work with you on the following options:

■   decision-making criteria;
■   priorities to formulate the business strategy, based on the organization's:
    – key strengths;
    – robust logic;
    – shared beliefs.

And another idea...

The beauty of the 'balanced business scorecard' is that it can be used immediately to take effective action that gives quick results. It can be based on a choice of methods. Whatever suits your business model best will be the most effective. This could be via one-to-one meetings; a research programme; off-site consultancy; facilitated group sessions – or a suitable combination of any of these.

The 'balanced business scorecard' process really works. It provides a common sense route to accelerated business development in difficult times.

7

Do the maths

It is easy to deceive yourself by making assumptions rather than calculations. Couple this with a tendency to immediately offer discounts when faced with tough times and you have recipe for disaster.

Consider some simple figures: you sell something for £100 and, with costs of £50, you are marking up by 100 per cent and making 50 per cent profit. Say you feel you must offer a discount. You want to make it significant to customers and yet preserve your profitability as much as possible, so you discount by 10 per cent. Thus your selling price is £90 and with costs still £50 you make £40 profit.

Now do one more calculation. What percentage of your profit has gone? £10 of your original £50 profit has gone – that's 20 per cent. This ratio gets even more scary when larger discounts are given.

We are not saying price reductions cannot be a part of your tough action; they may have to be. But...

Action

Always make such decisions after making careful calculations. Small discounts – 10 per cent, 12 per cent, 15 per cent may seem to do no great damage but sales increase must be achieved and often the amount of extra business needed just to retain the same overall profit is significant. Take care.

And another idea...

A number of accountants have calculation devices on their websites that will make this sort of calculation as you input a few key figures. Ask yours, look around or just type 'margin calculation' in Google.

8

Boost performance – motivate your people

Most managers would concede that motivation matters. Yet it takes thought and time, and good intentions evaporate like the morning mist when 'more pressing' matters interpose. Yet motivation – maximizing staff performance to ensure the achievement of planned results – is surely just as important in difficult times as in good. Indeed, there is a case for saying that it is more necessary; surely it is easier to perform when all is going well?

All managers are ultimately judged on their results. However many people you manage, you are dependent on the contribution of your team. And the quality of their contribution is dependent on their motivation. People perform better when their motivation is high. Furthermore, the difference between adequate and excellent performance spurred on by motivation can be considerable – and is just what you need in tough times.

Like most managers, you are doubtless busy. The greatest perceived difficulty about motivation is perhaps simply finding time to fit it in. Yet the rewards make the time it takes well worthwhile. It really does result in people achieving more, so the time needs to be put in to make sure people remain motivated, especially at times when performance matters most. Similarly, the problems of a demotivated team on their manager's time are all too obvious and again this is the last thing you want at a difficult time.

Successful managers are good at motivation in good times and in bad.

Action

What is most important, then? Without meaning to negate other factors, ten keys to successfully adopting a motivational management style may be summarized as follows:

1. Always think about the 'people' aspects of everything.

2. Keep a list of possible motivational actions, large and small, in mind.

3. Monitor the 'motivational temperature' regularly.

4. See the process as continuous and cumulative.

5. Ring the changes in terms of method to maintain interest.

6. Do not be censorious about what motivates others, either positively or negatively.

7. Beware of panaceas and easy options.

8. Make sufficient time for it.

9. Evaluate what works best within your team.

10. Remember that, in part at least, there should be a 'fun' aspect to work (and that it is your job to make sure this is so); maintaining this is especially important in difficult times. No one wants doom and gloom to pervade their whole working life.

Make motivation a habit, and make it effective, and you may be surprised by the results. The motivation for you to motivate others is in those results. Three things perhaps encapsulate what works best.

Motivational action must be:

- well judged – the right action, at the right time, carried out in an appropriate way;
- creative – finding new and different things to do as well as utilizing tried and tested methods;
- balanced – using a mixture of methods well matched to the individuals involved;
- continuous – motivation must be an inherent, ongoing part of management, not a 'when there is time' thing.

Having everyone performing well is always a sensible goal; in tough times it is a necessity and anything else is letting trouble in by default.

And another idea...

Finally, remember that the little things are as important as the large. Incentive payments may be powerful motivators (and, of course, incur no payment until the results are achieved), but so is saying 'Well done!' Have you used those words sufficiently often lately, and can you afford to neglect them when the situation makes doing so more difficult?

9

Tackling difficult issues – get uncomfortable

Some things cause difficulty at any time. In tough times they must be addressed. Let's be honest, however effective we may be, there are for most of us some tasks where our approach falters, where we are apt to procrastinate. When does this happen most often? On examination that is easy to say: certainly one example is when something is not just difficult, but when it is a particular kind of difficult – when it is actually uncomfortable. This may be conscious: for example, there may be things about your computer skills that mean action is delayed – knowing that your skills are not all they should be and being conscious that it is easy to get into deep trouble. Everyone probably has things that prompt such thoughts, and so delay action.

Alternatively, there are things where avoidance is a more subtle process, where we try to rationalize and do not actually accept that our procrastination is significant; sometimes refusing to see the reality at all. As a result things are left unaddressed and performance can deteriorate directly as a result. And all because of some half-buried and perhaps repressed feeling that taking action will be an uncomfortable experience. Consider an example.

The poor performer

Imagine: one of your staff is performing under par. This might be anything from not hitting sales targets to poor attendance; the details are unimportant. One thing is clear – it demands action and the rewards that follow are obvious. Dealing with it might produce more sales or higher productivity, say, depending on the precise details. Yet... with such things there can seem to be many reasons for delay. We think (or rather hope) that it will get better. We wait for other things: the end of the month (bringing further figures or evidence) or a forthcoming appraisal (which we know means we cannot put it off later than that). More than anything we blame other things. We are busy, we have greater priorities, or, even less convincingly, we are sorting other problems – fire fighting.

The truth is we do not want to deal with it. We may be unsure how to do so, and that can be awkward. More likely we do know what to do, but know it will be awkward or embarrassing to do so. Addressing it will take us into the discomfort zone, and we would rather distance ourselves, busying ourselves elsewhere (with something we designate 'more important'!) and remaining safely outside the zone of personal difficulty.

The facts of the matter are usually clear. It is not rocket science and we can usually deal with it if we address it. A poor performer is a good example. It is important, yet it is not complicated. Essentially only three options are possible. You can:

1. Put up with the poor performance, and allow it to continue (which is surely something no one would defend or recommend).
2. Address the problem with a determination to cure it, persuading or motivating someone to perform better; or training or developing the person to do whatever it is better, if their poor performance is due to a lack of some skill or competence.

3. Conclude, perhaps after option two has failed, that they will never get better and fire them (or otherwise move them to other areas of responsibility).

Both options two and three may be awkward. It is embarrassing to have to tell someone his or her performance is unacceptable, and most of us would find firing someone worse. So, action is delayed.

Action

Get real. The situation here needs to be addressed head-on. Such a situation is not a failing of logic, not a deficit of information or understanding, or anything else that mistakenly leads us away from the sensible and necessary course – it is a personal decision: we put avoiding personal discomfort above sorting the problem out, and, very likely, delay makes the problem worse.

Before you say 'But I would never make that kind of decision', consider further. If this thinking is partly subconscious, then that is likely so because we push it into the back of our mind, refusing to really analyse what is occurring, or simply allowing other activity to create a blinding smokescreen. Now let us think more constructively. Which elements of your work are likely to run foul of this kind of avoidance technique? Dealing with poor performance has already been cited as an example. Others include:

- raising a difficult issue at a meeting (it gets put off rather than risking controversy or argument);
- cold calling (many of us should do more, but it is not our favourite thing);

▪ networking (sounds good: we all hope to meet people at that conference we attend, then come out with one business card because we are not quite sure how to approach people);
▪ chasing debtors (we hate it, avoid it or do it half heartedly and so cash flow suffers; yet we all recognize that it is not an order until the money is in the bank);
▪ follow up (when the customer has said 'I'll think about it', how many times do we make one perfunctory phone call to be told they are in a meeting, then leave it so long that the moment passes because we are not quite sure what to say next time?).

Such things (some of which are investigated elsewhere in this book) are, to an extent, routine. Others may be more personal, linking to a particular skill or activity. For instance:

▪ avoiding presentations, even when they offer promotional opportunity, because 'It's not really my thing';
▪ avoiding sitting on a committee where you might make valuable contacts because meetings are in the evening and 'It's not fair on the family.'

You may well be able to extend the list in both categories (be honest, as we said at the beginning).

An active search for opportunity

So, what do we conclude from this? There is a significant opportunity here. You need to resolve to actively seek out uncomfortable situations. You need to see the discomfort zone as an attractive place to go. Somewhere where you can achieve action and influence results, and often do so quickly and easily. After all, probably most people can identify with this feeling: you take some long-overdue action, find – however momentarily distasteful it may be doing it – that it changes things for the better and end up saying 'I just wish I had done that sooner.'

If you find yourself putting things off in future try a moment's analysis and you may find that action more likely follows. Take a systematic approach:

- Spot the areas needing action that you are in danger of failing to address.
- Ask yourself why you are turning away from something and check specifically that it is not simply to avoid personal discomfort.
- Check that action is possible. Do you know what to do? Do you have the skills to do it?
- Fill any information or skills gap, taking time so to do if necessary (this is usually time well spent; for example if you fire someone without checking out the employment legislation situation you may make a small hole very deep).
- Programme action into your list of 'things to do', giving matters their true priority and having worked out what you have to gain (after all, you deserve some motivation if you are going to choose to be uncomfortable).
- Take the action and take note: if it solves the problem, generates the opportunity – whatever – learn from it for next time.

And another idea...

Make this approach a habit. Make entering the discomfort zone a catchphrase. This approach is the antidote to things happening by default. It needs some resolve, but here is truly a technique that, overriding an undesirable element of human nature, provides a quick, simple, sure way to increase your effectiveness in tough times.

10

Time management – focus on key issues

Too much to do? So little time? Does this sound familiar? When things get tough business-wise, you probably feel under even more pressure to get more and more done in less and less time. But is this really what effective time management is about?

Time management is essentially about tasks – achieving output, being more effective and delivering results. You probably don't make a list of what you do every day but you know how busy you are. But think about tasks versus time – perhaps you have no difficulty in being industrious, but you need to manage your time better. It is often easier to measure the activity when you should be measuring the outcome. Good time management means working out what (action) produces the best result. You should not confuse being 'busy' with 'output'.

One of the best ways of achieving good time management is to work smarter, not harder. Easy enough to say, but by learning a few good time management habits, your output will increase hugely.

Action

1. Avoid procrastination. If it's urgent – do it now! Don't put off doing something that must be done. Quite often something that really needs sorting out immediately can be done quickly. If your office building is on fire it doesn't take long to call the emergency services. It might take a while to put the fire out, but that isn't your job.

    Important tasks take much longer. That is because an important task is something that requires consideration, thought and possibly involves taking advice from others. Quite often important tasks are put off because you know they will take up too much time. If you don't deal with them and make time to deal with them, things will not go well in future.

    Don't overdo tasks you enjoy so that, by taking up your time, prevent you starting a less enjoyable piece of work. This is a common failing. If you like doing something you may allow yourself to take far longer over it than something you dislike. It is one of the easiest ways for people to waste time, but not many are honest enough to admit that they do it. But this author (FK) is guilty as charged.

2. Do it now. Learn to prioritize. On your 'to do' list (you do have one, don't you?) itemize tasks in order of urgency or importance. If you don't know which tasks should be tackled in which order of importance, follow these guidelines.

    Become a list-freak. Make a list of everything you need to do. Annotate the tasks – category A and B. Tear the list in half and throw away the list of B tasks. Take the list of A tasks and look at it again. Split it into two categories – A and B. Discard the list B and work on the A tasks until they are done.

3. Why be perfect? You are probably more than familiar with the Pareto Principle – the 80/20 rule. Sometimes almost perfect is good enough. Usually it is more important to have a report you have agreed to produce on the desk, in time for a meeting, and containing the information needed, than taking a couple of hours to tinker around with the presentation until you feel it is 100 per cent perfect.

    In the same way, most people will get 80 per cent of their results from 20 per cent of their time. Watch how you spend your time – in the office, with customers, attending to staff queries, dealing with interruptions. Twenty per cent of your day is spent on important tasks, while the rest – a staggering 80 per cent of the day – just gets used up.

    You can apply this model across the board: 20 per cent of customers produce 80 per cent of the business. Look at that in terms of dealing with difficult situations – should you start getting tough with some of your time-wasters?

4. Zap interruptions. One of the easiest ways to waste time is to allow other people to interrupt you when you are busy. You need to be strict with your time, without being rude. Of course, you can't just slam the door in someone's face, shout 'Go away!' (even if you would like to), or completely blank them when they approach you. However, you could create a 'buffer' zone. Don't commit to a meeting or accept an invitation the moment you are asked. Be vague – play for time. Say that you must check your schedule and how it interfaces with other people. If you're able to just say 'No', do so politely and with a smile.

    Many people find this very difficult. You don't want to offend someone. You feel you should make the effort. It won't hurt, just this once. But if you cannot learn to say

'No', how can anyone work out the value of your saying 'Yes'?

One way of avoiding interruptions is to allow technology to take the strain. Use the 'off' switch on your telephone, or let the auto answer take over. It's quite easy to let the phone ring and go to voice mail. You don't have to check every text message that comes in. Neither do e-mails need opening the second they appear on your computer screen. Make it a rule not to look at them more than twice a day – around noon and again before you leave your workplace for the day.

5. Practise some good time management habits. Do you know people who boast about being avid multi-taskers? This probably means that they actually do lots of things – but, er, none of them all that well. Try to do one thing (well) at a time. There is nothing more satisfying than crossing a job off your list.

   If you're involved in a complex task that is taking a long time, progress it as far as you possibly can. Then leave it until it can be continued with, you've received the information you're waiting for, or hand it over to someone else who is involved in the process.

6. Paperwork – the five-way detox. Is paperwork the bane of your life? If so, the five-way detox may suit you:
   - make sure you *deal* with it only once;
   - *determine* it – decide on a future action – do not put it back on the pile;
   - *delegate* it to another person;
   - *deposit* it in a file;
   - *discard* it – dump it in the bin.

And another idea...

Five ways to create time in a week:

1. Get yourself organized. You can't achieve anything if you're in a muddle.
2. Deal with difficult tasks – now. Don't just shelve them. Problems don't go away; if ignored they just get worse.
3. Ban interruptions.
4. Become a clutter buster – clear desk, clear mind.
5. Do one thing at a time – finish one task before you start another.

Finally, if you want something done – ask a busy person...

11

Check staff
employment contracts

If your business is going through a shake-up or a rough time, it's possible you may have to down-size in the near future. Whether it is related to a recession, or other reasons, it pays to know where you stand in terms of your employment contracts.

Should times prove exceptionally difficult, redundancies may become inevitable. But you can keep this from being a crisis if you are sensible, keep your head and deal with people in a sensitive fashion. You must follow the legal framework as it is laid down.

It could be financially punitive to your company if you aren't aware of the size of the lump sum payments for redundancy that would have to be made to dismissed employees. These payments should be given at the time the employees leave the organization. You must take care over dismissal, otherwise you could end up facing an employment tribunal.

Technically, redundancy means dismissal from employment caused by an employer's need to reduce his or her workforce. Redundancy may happen because a workplace is closing down, relocating, has been sold to another organization or because fewer employees are needed for a particular kind of work.

If a job is not continuing, this is regarded as redundancy. It is not redundancy if you dismiss someone only immediately to take on a direct replacement. An employer is permitted to recruit more workers but it has to be for a different kind of work, or in another location (at which place employment has already been offered to the person being made redundant which they have refused to accept).

Action

1. Consult your human resources department and look carefully at the employment contracts for those employees facing possible redundancy. Your human resources staff should be able to advise you on technicalities, or for safety consult an employment lawyer.

2. Certain categories of persons are not eligible for redundancy payments. These include members of the armed forces; House of Lords and House of Commons staff and apprentices whose service ends at the end of the apprenticeship contract.

3. If you realize that redundancies will be needed, you can ask for volunteers. An employee will qualify for a redundancy payment if he/she volunteers, as long as an employer actually formally dismisses them.

And another idea...

You are legally obliged to put the dismissal in writing. This need not be a formal letter although it must state the facts. You can also express sympathy and regret, and thank the person for their loyalty and hard work over the years. Redundancy knocks a person's self-esteem – so make an effort to minimize the hurt if possible.

12

Check employment contracts (for the employee)

Your company may be struggling in a tough economic climate. You may fear that they will be downsizing in the near future. It is only sensible to know your rights, whether things stay on track or (as could happen) get worse. This is true whatever your position; don't let seniority blind you to the dangers.

In terms of your employment contract, as an employee, the more information you have, the less likely you are to be greeted by an unwelcome surprise. It would be rather unwelcome news if, when given notice to leave your employment, you begin dreaming of the nice, fat lump-sum payment you'll receive only to find you're not eligible for redundancy for some reason.

Technically, redundancy means dismissal from employment caused by the employer's need to reduce his or her workforce. Redundancy may happen because a workplace is closing down, relocating, has been sold to another organization or because fewer employees are needed for a particular kind of work.

Your job must have disappeared for it to be regarded as redundancy. It is not redundancy if your employer immediately takes on a direct replacement for you. Your employer may be recruiting more workers but it has to be for a different kind of work, or in another location (at which place employment has already been offered to you but you have refused).

Action

1. If you don't already have a copy of your contract, ask your human resources department for one. Study its terms.

2. You are entitled to a lump-sum payment if you are made redundant and have had at least two years' continuous service with the company.

3. You will receive a redundancy payment only if you are working under a contract of employment. The self-employed and members of a partnership do not qualify under the Employment Act, though they may have separate contractual agreements.

4. In general, to be eligible for a redundancy payment you must have been dismissed by your employer rather than resigned from your job. The reason for the dismissal must have been redundancy.

5. The amount of the lump-sum redundancy payment depends on: how long you have been continuously employed by your employer; how your years of continuous service relate to a particular age band; and your weekly pay, up to a legal limit.

6. If you are laid off, or put on short time (ie you receive less than half a week's pay) for four weeks in a row or six weeks out of 13, you may also claim a redundancy payment without waiting to be dismissed for redundancy.

7. You must make your claim in writing to your employer. Your employer may refuse to accept it if they believe normal working is likely to resume within four weeks.

8. If you are on a fixed-term contract and it ends without being renewed, this counts as a dismissal, and you may under these circumstances be due a redundancy payment.

9. You are able to apply to an employment tribunal if you disagree with your employer about your entitlement to a redundancy payment. You can do this at any time as long as it is within six months of the date of your leaving employment.

And another idea...

If you've been given notice of dismissal because of redundancy, you are entitled to reasonable time off from your employer, with pay, during working hours. This is on condition you use that time to look for another job or make arrangements for training for future employment – it's not just for meeting friends, having coffee and a gossip.

13

Cut down on travel

Let us be clear at the outset – some travel may be as necessary in tough times as any other, but thousands of journeys must be undertaken every day that are not really necessary. All over the world taxis, cars, trains and aeroplanes are taking people to places and to see people when the transaction could be handled some other way. The attendant cost and time cannot even be guessed at, but saving this time and money helps directly in tough times. To be entirely honest, if a business opportunity presents itself to travel to a city such as New York, Singapore or London, or to attend a conference at a well-known resort area, it is very tempting to attend, despite the fact that overseas and long distance travel can be very hard work. So the first rule in this area is not to undertake journeys purely on the basis of your personal pleasure or as an escape from dealing with tough issues.

Action

Where some form of direct contact is necessary, always consider the alternatives, and resist the desire to meet face-to-face; even a trip from one side of a city to another is time consuming.

- *Have people come to you:* this may be possible – you may only have to suggest it or it may even be worth footing the bill and providing an overnight hotel stay; this will cost you no more than if you travelled in the reverse direction, and will save you time.

- Send someone else: yes, even to that attractively located conference – consider delegating.

- *Telephone:* some things really can be dealt with pretty simply and you do not need to meet face-to-face. An initial telephone contact gets things started, with a visit coming later if necessary (and mobile phones increase the options). Remember that telephone conversations do not provide a written record.

- Write or e-mail: this will provide you with a written record but, like the telephone, may not generate such immediate or accurate understanding as a meeting.

- *Use technology:* for those able to afford it, modern telecommunications offer increasingly sophisticated possibilities, including telephone and video conferencing where you can be linked electronically to a group of people all able to converse and see each other.

- Reduce costs: travel costs vary widely. Check advance booking possibilities, travel at the most economic time, on an economic carrier and in a 'suitable' class. For example, business class is clearly more comfortable on long haul flights, but you pay a huge premium; maybe an extra night to get over the jet lag would be better – and less costly.

And another idea...

Policy is important here, so too is setting an example. If everyone uses second class rail travel for the duration, say, then the impact on a cost-cutting campaign and the thinking that goes with it will be greater. If everyone travels economy class *except* directors, this may simply cause resentment. Maybe you could link your travel policy to a suggestions scheme for making other savings.

In an organization of any size the implications here are considerable. So before booking, think for a moment. Of course some things can genuinely only be dealt with face-to-face and some journeys are essential – but not all.

14

Negotiate to get costs down

Let us be clear. Negotiation and persuasion are different things. They are certainly interrelated: successful persuasion gains agreement to action (to buy perhaps), whereas negotiation is concerned with identifying, arranging and agreeing the terms and conditions that accompany agreement. Agreement must logically come first. People do not waste time negotiating something in which they have no interest.

So, if negotiation is about the terms and conditions on which a deal is struck, then it becomes a prime technique to deploy in difficult economic times, in particular:

■ to ensure you get the best deal from your suppliers, something that impacts directly on costs;
■ to secure good deals with customers, especially major customers who can be very demanding in the terms they specify.

For instance, if a retail customer demands delivery to ten regional centres instead of one, asks for special packing and throws in a request for promotional assistance, it is going to cost. Unchallenged, such things may reduce margins damagingly.

Action

Negotiation is a complex process. The complexity comes from the need to orchestrate a many-faceted process rather than because of any element being individually intellectually taxing. But you need to be quick on your feet to keep all the necessary balls in the air, and always see the broad picture while concentrating on individual details.

To take action and gain from negotiation you must understand how it works. Negotiation must not turn into an argument (or an impasse usually results), but it is adversarial. Both parties want the best deal possible. Yet compromise is essential: stick out for the perfect deal and the other party may walk away. Give way too easily and you will regret what is then agreed. What is sought is the so-called win–win outcome, where both parties are satisfied and, while neither may have their ideal 'best deal', they each have an agreement about which they feel comfortable.

Negotiation has a ritual aspect. A process needs to be gone through, and it takes time. There is to-and-fro debate, and it must be seen that a mutually agreeable solution is being sought. Too much haste, a rush for agreement or a take-it-or-leave-it approach can fail simply because the other party does not feel that the process is being taken sufficiently seriously. They look for hidden meaning, believe that something better must be possible and again the outcome can be stalemate.

Because of these factors the best negotiators are careful to take the broad view, to understand the other person's viewpoint and what they are trying to achieve and why. Because the issues and motivations of negotiation are complex, the way it is handled is important. In addition, the negotiator who seems confident, dealing with all the issues logically and managing the overall process as well as picking up the detail, commands respect. How do you get on top of it all to this extent? Well, beyond having a clear understanding of the process, the key is preparation. You cannot wing it.

First things first

The rule about preparation is simple. Do it. Preparation may only be a grand term for the age-old advice that it is best to engage the brain before the mouth, and it may take only a few moments. Of course, alternatively it may mean sitting round the table with a few colleagues thrashing out exactly how to proceed with something. Whatever is necessary, it should always happen.

Clear objectives are vital. Simply saying 'I want the best deal possible' provides nothing tangible with which to work. There is all the difference in the world between an author saying 'Let's see if the editor will pay me more for my next article' and aiming to obtain a 10 per cent fee increase. Planning should be designed to produce the equivalent of a route map, something that helps shape the meeting. With people it is just not possible to predict everything exactly as it will happen. However, your plan should provide both an ideal route forward and a basis to help if things do not go exactly to plan.

A final point may also encourage you to spend time preparing. You must appear well prepared. If you seem unfamiliar with the issues then it is more likely you will lose out in the negotiation. Preparation is the foundation to success and provides insurance against being outclassed.

The core element

The core of the negotiation process revolves around what are called variables: factors that can be dealt with in different ways to create various deals. Thus in negotiating price, say, the price itself is clearly a variable, but discussion may involve associated matters such as payment terms, expenses, delivery, and other factors such as timing, staffing and more.

The overall rules here include:

- aiming high, going for the best deal possible;
- discovering the full list of variables the other person has in mind;
- treating everything as a potential variable;
- dealing with detail within the total picture (rather than one point at a time without reference to others).

Different ways of using variables can increase the power from which you deal. For instance, you can prompt attention by offering reward: something you are prepared to give. Conversely you can offer punishment: by flagging your intention to withhold something. Your case is strengthened, given legitimacy in the jargon, by being supported by factual evidence, or by the use of bogeys, peripheral factors included only to distract or seek sympathy.

You have to rank the variables, in preparation and in fine-tuning as you go, identifying things that are:

- essential: you cannot agree any deal without these points being part of it;
- ideal: what you intend to achieve (and the priorities, because there may be more of these than it is realistic to achieve);
- tradable: in other words those things that you are prepared to give away to help create a workable deal.

The concept of trading variables is key to negotiation. Aim never to give anything away. Concessions (variables given away) must be traded. Thus a computer consultant might link two aspects of their cost to their client, saying, 'We can certainly make sure all rail travel cost is at second class rates, but we do need to add a little to the fees for the travel time.' In trading, the value of every concession must be maximized when you give it –

and minimized when you accept it. Thus saying, 'I suppose I could do that, though it will make more work, but okay', makes it seem that what you are agreeing to is worth more than perhaps it is. Saying something like 'I would never normally do this' implies you are making an exception in their favour. And saying 'Well, I suppose if I do that you won't need to...' exemplifies the effect that the concession has for them. Clearly how such things are said, perhaps incorporating some exaggeration, affects their reception.

Similarly you should try to minimize the other parties' concessions in the same way. These can be dismissed – 'Fine, now next...', belittled – 'Well, that's a small point out of the way', amortized – 'I suppose that saves a little each month', taken for granted – 'I would certainly expect that' or otherwise reduced in power by the way they are accepted and referred to during the discussion.

So, discussion has to be planned, directed and controlled. The confidence you display during such a discussion is significant (and links back to preparation). You must be clear about what you want to achieve. If you utilize every possible aspect of the discussion and treat it as a variable, and deploy appropriate techniques to balance the whole picture and arrive at where you want to be (or somewhere close), then you can achieve a reasonable outcome. Remember the win–win scenario. The job is not to take people to the cleaners. Only being prepared to agree something that is weighted heavily in your favour means negotiation may be more likely to break down and no agreement at all may result. Indeed, you must recognize that sometimes walking away, rather than agreeing something you cannot live with, is the right decision.

Even when you have someone over the proverbial barrel, a widely skewed deal often makes no sense. You need to think long term. How will screwing them into the ground make you look? What are the future consequences? What may happen next time if your case is weaker?

And another idea...

Do not underestimate the individual techniques that can be deployed. A confident negotiator may use many different ploys to enhance their case. Some are simple, but may still add power. One example will illustrate this – the use of silence, which many find embarrassing, and feel obliged to make a point or a response. Too often someone will ask something like 'How important is this to you?' They wait a moment and then continue – 'Well, I'm sure it must be an important factor, now let's...'. Such a comment produces no real impact and, more important, no information. Wait – wait a long time if necessary (try counting to yourself; a pause that seems long and unsustainable may be only a few seconds long). But using – really using – silence is one significant ploy that can help ensure a response, provide information and assist the whole nego-tiating process.

If you negotiate well you can gain considerably, not least finan-cially. Indeed a review of your agreements with suppliers and other arrangements when economic times are changing may be very useful.

15

Have a (personal) escape plan

This chapter is unashamedly personal. You must accept that the worst can happen (often regardless of seniority), and if the organization you work for does founder, or even just wobble, redundancies may be inevitable. Whatever else you accept or reject reading this book, accept this. The organization can function without you. Yes, it is almost unthinkable – until you think about it. Common sense then tells you that it is true. So what does this mean?

Action

This situation implies action on two fronts. First, tough times tend to increase the workload, and maybe the stress, too, but it is very much a time to watch the signs – and your back. Things can creep up on you; as the old saying has it, it is difficult to see the writing on the wall when your back's to it. At worst, one minute you are working away, saving the company single-handedly, the next you are reading your redundancy notice.

Being watchful may allow you to:

- avoid such a fate;
- be forewarned of it in a way that gives you more time to respond (and check your contract);
- leave the sinking ship ahead of what you may see as a looming, untenable situation.

Second, you need to make sure that you are in a state of job-moving readiness. This means making sure that:

- you check the terms of your contract;
- your curriculum vitae is up to date;
- you have a clear idea what direction you would want to look in if a move is forced upon you, and of how to go about making the move;
- contacts that normal career management realities suggest are kept fresh, are indeed fresh even when you are busier than usual (see also Chapter 36 on networking).

Sadly, this is good advice whatever level you work at, however long you have been with an organization and however much you may see yourself as fireproof and invaluable. The trouble with unpredictable events is that they are, well, unpredictable. Faced with emergency action of this sort don't find your first thought is, 'I should have seen it coming.'

And another idea...

The scenario described above also means that there may be things you want to do to keep yourself up to date and fit for the job market. This might mean a range of things from reading a business book to attending a course or taking on some project designed to give you a certain type of experience. You have been warned.

16

Small can be beautiful – shedding people

Times are tough, we know. You may have been tasked with the responsibility of making redundancies in your department. This is not an easy job at the best of times. In a difficult economic climate it is critical that you can justify your method of selecting people for redundancy. There is no way anyone, these days, can be seen to be guilty of bias.

Making employees redundant is an emotive and delicate issue so an unemotional and professional approach is needed. It is assumed here that any cost-cutting that might reduce the need for making people redundant has already been done – cutting salaries, postponing bonuses or reducing staff costs in other ways. If there is no alternative, selecting the right candidates for dismissal is nerve-wracking at the very least. For both legal and personal reasons you need to be absolutely clear in your mind that you are being completely fair.

Action

You need to balance up the factors that you can legitimately take into account when tasked with laying people off. When seeking what constitutes reasonable grounds, the following points should be considered:

1. Length of service is an important factor. You may use it as your main reason – 'last in – first out'.

2. Often financial reasons are behind the need for redundancies, in which case it is possible that the most expensive employees may have to go. But consider this: the longest serving people could be an asset the organization cannot afford to lose. They are loyal employees and good at what they do. The best course of action here is to ask them if they would consider staying on but agree to a pay cut.

3. Should someone's skills, or lack of them, be a criterion for redundancy, this could be the justification for laying them off. However, if their skills aren't relevant to the issue, it won't form sufficient grounds for dismissal.

4. You may have to consider an employee's performance. In order for it to stand as an appropriate reason for making someone redundant, you will have to be able to demonstrate clearly that the person's performance is poor and below the acceptable standard for continued employment.

5. Someone could be selected for redundancy on the grounds of their attendance record or because of their attitude or behaviour. Should they have a poor disciplinary record this reason could also uphold a decision to dismiss someone.

6. Look at things from a personal angle – what will the effect of redundancy be on the people who get laid off? They may be without work for some time. They may have difficulty maintaining payments on their home. Perhaps they will not be able to get further employment without taking a pay cut. Getting another job might mean they need to relocate, which could involve children in chang-

ing schools or a spouse giving up their job. Consider whether there may be other staff for whom redundancy may not have such dramatic consequences. This approach can soften the negative impact of redundancy on the organization's image.

The action can be swift – clear your desk and go at the end of the week – but the terms should always be as generous as possible (people talk – to each other, to the press...). Whatever you do, don't forget to complete all necessary documentation. Deal with people as if you will want to re-hire them (you might). That leaves them likely to want to rejoin you. Consider initiating effective handovers: some work done by those leaving may need to continue. This must be picked up smoothly.

And another idea...

If you're an employer looking to shed employees, bear in mind that at the very least someone facing redundancy needs to be given as much notice as possible. People have a right to know if there is a threat of redundancy hanging over them. They need to plan their options in good time in case they are one of the ones being laid off. Honesty on the employer's part is always the best policy. Be up-front and tell your team/department that, for example, four redundancies are required, but that final decisions will not be taken for another three months. If you show sensitivity towards your employees, you will find the process is likely to go ahead more smoothly. There could even be a silver lining to all this: once 'dead wood' is cleared away you may find those left in place are renewed with enthusiasm and a leaner organization can have a new lease of life once the tough times finally recede.

17

Staff – delegating tasks

Managing people in tough times is not easy, but it has to be done. When things are bumpy economically, it is essential that your staff perform to their usual standard, if not better. When trying to get the most out of people, you need to enable them to work to the uppermost level of their competence. This requires good delegation skills, and if you haven't had much training in this sphere it is difficult to do just off the cuff. In terms of effective management organization, good delegation is critical to developing and improving performance in others.

Delegation is a word that is bandied about liberally and something that people pay lip service to. People rarely delegate effectively. Mostly what happens is that people get told to do a job or take something on – that is not delegation. Very often it is an either/or situation. Either they get dumped with something they can't cope with or they don't get a chance to prove their worth because delegation is not implemented effectively. More often than not it hasn't been thought through. This results in things going wrong, breakdowns, upsets and so on. This is all very demotivating for staff and managers alike, and is even worse when the organization is facing a tough future.

Action

How to assign or allocate work to staff

Balance the work that has to be done against the availability of people and their skills. Bear in mind that some tasks may be routine and repetitive, some may not.

When you assign work to someone you can retain the decision-making responsibility, should it become necessary to decide upon an alternative course of action. Delegation can, if you wish, go one step further and hand authority to make decisions to the team member.

Reasons not to delegate

The most frequent excuse is: 'It's easier to do it myself.' All that happens here is overload for you and loss of morale for others. The reasons for not wishing to delegate usually are:

- you do not understand the need to delegate or do not know how to do it;

- you lack confidence in team members, and therefore will not give them the authority for decision-making;

- you have tried to delegate in the past, but failed and so will not try again;

- you like doing a particular job that should be delegated, but will not delegate it even though you know the team member would enjoy the job;

- you do not understand the management role or how to go about it;

- you are frightened of making yourself dispensable, so keep hold of every job.

Delegation is a skill

Like most skills, they can be learned. Here are some tips for effective delegation:

■ Plan delegation well in advance.

■ Think through exactly what you want done. Define a precise aim.

■ Consider the degree of guidance and support needed by delegate.

■ Pitch the briefing appropriately. Check understanding.

■ Establish review dates. Check understanding.

■ Establish a 'buffer' period at the end, in which failings can be put right.

■ Delegate whole jobs wherever possible, rather than bits and pieces.

■ Inform others involved.

■ Having delegated, stand back. Do not 'hover'.

■ Recognize that the work may not be done exactly as you would have done it.

■ Do not 'nit-pick'.

■ Delegate, do not abdicate responsibility.

Things that can be delegated

■ work that should be done by another person or in another department;

■ time-consuming tasks not entailing much decision making;

■ repetitive tasks that require decision making and could help develop a team member.

The best way forward is to set a delegation plan and timetable. It can take something like eight to twelve times longer to delegate a job effectively as it can to actually do it – believe it or not, it's true. But if you take the time to delegate properly in the first place you will save yourself far more time in the future.

Tasks that should not be delegated:

- seeking opportunities for the enterprise;
- setting strategic aims and objectives;
- creating high achievement plans for the department;
- co-ordinating activity – knowing the task that has to be done, the abilities and needs of the staff, the resources available and mixing them to achieve optimum results;
- communicating with staff and with senior managers and colleagues;
- the training and development of your team.

If you can free yourself to do the jobs that you alone can do, you will be managing well in difficult times.

How to delegate

Each task that has been chosen as suitable for delegation should have a specification. This should state clearly:

- the objective or intended goal of the job;
- the method you have developed to do it;
- data requirements and where/who the information comes from;
- any aids or equipment needed to accomplish the task;
- definition of boundaries of responsibility;
- principal categories of decisions that have to be made;
- any limitations on authority where making these decisions are concerned.

When you are ready, coaching or training of the delegate can begin. Keep track as you delegate jobs to staff and monitor the process closely at first. As things progress, you can loosen your grip to simply ensuring that the job continues to be done properly.

And another idea...

Delegation is often considered a one-way ticket, being helpful only to the person in charge. But it has a bonus effect: it is of considerable benefit to the member of staff to whom the work is delegated. Effective delegation is a huge boost to the development of individuals both practically and psychologically. Win–win!

18

Image and presentation count

Even though we are dealing with tough issues in difficult times, an important aspect of how you and your business will be perceived when going through a rough patch is how you present yourself. This section serves as a reminder about creating the right impression, building confidence and maintaining self-esteem. If you can keep your head (and your shirt well-ironed) when all about you are losing theirs... as the saying goes. This may sound a bit fluffy, but it isn't. Don't underestimate how important it is to make a favourable impression even when, because of business being particularly hard hit, it's an effort to do so.

Within a few moments, assumptions and judgements are made. You know it's true – we all do it. If your organization is struggling, there is nothing more demoralizing than looking around to see colleagues shuffling about in disconsolate fashion with miserable faces. However hard you try to avoid doing so, you (and anyone visiting your offices – be they customers, suppliers or others) are likely to make an instant decision about how things are going in the organization because of the way its employees look, speak or dress. The statistics speak for themselves about what people notice when you meet them:

- 55 per cent of the impression made is how you look – posture and what you wear;
- 38 per cent is the energy and enthusiasm – body language, tone of voice;
- only 7 per cent is what you actually say to a person.

Visual impressions are more important than oral messages. You may be going to the bank manager or your financial backers or shareholders to report on the current state of the business. Those first few seconds when you enter the room could be crucial. Looking scruffy and down at heel may be one way of going about it (if you think playing the sympathy card will work). But looking professional and well held-together is likely to get you off to a good start. Everything you do afterwards will become just that much easier. A positive beginning not only affects any business that may transpire, it affects your confidence too. Confidence requires preparation and needs to be actively worked on to ensure you achieve the right impact.

Action

Things to watch out for

This isn't a matter of tricks or gimmicks. It's about being business-like and professional. People are more likely to respond positively to your requests if you look well presented.

Weak posture is a dead give-away, as is negative body language. Something even as simple as slouching at your desk is a bad habit. It not only looks awful but you are likely to have back trouble later on, if you don't try to sit and stand up straight. One tip from the experts is to imagine 'a golden thread' running from the top of your head to the ceiling. When you stand or sit, imagine this thread is pulling you upright. You will grow taller and instantly be more noticeable.

Watch out for any indicators of nervousness or low self-confidence in yourself and others. This could include fidgeting, covering your mouth with your hand, tightly clasped hands, bowed head and avoiding eye contact. The way people control their arms gives powerful clues as to how confident, open and receptive they are. Keeping your arms relaxed and to the side of your body shows you are not scared. You give the impression of being able to take whatever comes your way – meeting things head-on.

Looking the part

If you want to be seen as a confident and self-assured person, capable of conducting business negotiations in a cool professional manner, using open body language will make you more persuasive. Stand upright, balanced on both feet with your weight evenly distributed. If you can pull in those abdominals, you'll look not only taller but slimmer. Remember, your body is an instrument – it can convey every emotion.

Another tip is mirroring gestures. It's great for creating a good first impression with people you need to impress. By copying what the other person does, it endorses the favourable view they've formed of you.

Actions speak louder than words – body language speaks volumes

When you are trying to create a favourable impression with someone, your body will quite naturally point towards them – your face, hands, arms, feet and legs. These gestures can be quite subconscious. But they are picked up easily by the other person.

Try watching next time you've got a few moments to spare – observe how individuals position themselves when communicating with each other. You'll notice how they naturally angle themselves towards the person with whom they are trying to create rapport, and turn away from those who they are seeking to avoid.

Eye contact

Making the correct sort of eye contact in tricky business negotiations is important. It could be a crucial meeting and as is often the case, you are probably dealing with someone you don't know very well. Here are a few things to remember.

It is quite natural to look at people eye to eye and across the top of the nose. This is the safe area, to which eye contact should be confined. It's possible to relax and widen the area of vision in social situations, but at work keep your gaze within the appropriate limit.

If you're very nervous try not to stare obsessively at someone when they are speaking to you. This is disconcerting at the very least. On the other hand, looking away completely, slow blinking or closing the eyes for longer periods than normal, can be a clear indication of lack of interest, or worse, boredom.

If you're finding it difficult to maintain someone's interest in what you are saying, gestures can direct eye contact. Point to something you are talking about. As the other person directs his eyes towards it, he will lift his head and you will be able to engage eye contact again. This may help to change the emphasis of your meeting.

Creating impact

Another aspect of good presentation when you are trying to keep everything under control is creating the right impact. It's important at the best of times, but it is crucial when dealing with tough situations at work. The way you dress should where possible show authority and inspire confidence. But don't forget you need to express approachability too. Be clear about the image you want to create. Don't be fussy – the aim here is to be remembered positively.

We aren't talking about the latest trends in fashion. Clothes do matter but it's far safer to be well groomed and somewhat conservative. Remember, it's far more important to have well-manicured hands, clean, well-cut hair and good quality accessories. If the overall impression given is that you look as if you care about your appearance, you will subconsciously put out signals that other aspects of your work/life are in reasonable shape too.

One of the quickest (and cheapest) ways to win people over is to smile. You probably have a pleasant natural smile. Often, due to nervousness or apprehension, all that seems to register on someone's face are the stress muscles. A smile lights up a face – and lightens the tone of the exchange. People who smile give the impression of being at ease, sincere and confident. It relaxes those with whom you are making contact.

If you have an appointment, be punctual. On a first meeting the overriding effect should be that you are capable of arriving somewhere on time. If you turn up late, whatever the reason and however genuine the excuse, the impression you give is a negative one. However organized you are, allow yourself extra time if you are travelling to an appointment, to avoid stress. Appearing cool, calm and collected is well worth the extra investment of a taxi ride, if that's all it takes.

Pay attention!

This may sound like unnecessary advice, but it's surprising how many people can't stop their eyes straying when someone walks past an office or a commotion takes place outside. Keep your eyes and ears directed towards the person with whom you are communicating at all times. You must prove that they have all your attention, because when times are difficult you may only have a few minutes of their time.

Remember to switch off your mobile phone. There's no better way to kill off goodwill at a business meeting than being interrupted by an unwanted bleeping coming from your pocket or bag. Never compound the sin by answering your phone – instant disaster. This applies the other way round too. If your business contact has the insensitivity to receive calls and messages throughout your meeting, it's an insult. It shows a lack of respect for you and creates completely the wrong impression.

There are occasions when such interruptions are unavoidable. If you are about to start an important conversation, have the courtesy to mention that you are expecting a phone message (hopefully with some information that is relevant to the meeting). When the phone does ring, explain politely that it is the call you'd been expecting, and could they excuse you for a moment while you respond. Make a discreet exit and be brief.

In summary – consider a little self-analysis

Get some feedback from others on how they see you. Ask yourself and a few trusted friends these questions:

- In what situations and on what occasions that you currently face do you most lack confidence? Create a list.

- What kind of image do you currently project?

- What impression do you make on people at a first meeting?

- How do people who know you well react towards you?

- What one behavioural trait might be worth changing to create a more positive effect at work in the current economic climate?

It doesn't matter who you are, people will make judgements about you based on their first impressions. One of the key reasons why you need to spend time and effort on your personal presentation in tough times is to give yourself a confidence boost. If you know you look good and behave well you'll feel more self-assured.

Remember the four main areas

■ good posture, natural smile;

■ clothing – flattering and appropriate;

■ overall impression – well groomed, professional, under-stated;

■ be polite and rely on your own unique strengths.

And another idea...

The outcome of many difficult encounters is often determined by the composure of the parties involved. A lack of skill or knowledge may go unnoticed but a conflict can be resolved or a business deal won purely through a display of confidence.

Self-belief and self-assurance are vital if you are to realize your potential. This will help to maximize your chances for business success when times are tough. By reviewing your personal image and presentation skills you can increase your self-confidence. This has a beneficial effect on your colleagues and others around you both personally and professionally.

Not giving customers an inch

Customers are important. If Heaven and Earth need moving to keep them happy, then we move them; usually without argument and especially when we are desperate to hang onto them. But is this always right? Is it right in tough times?

Consider the downsides: first, in the heartland of your work area. Say someone is recommending software for a particular application. The client bemoans the cost of the recommendation. They plead for a cheaper option. Under pressure you give in, you recommend – albeit grudgingly – something less, albeit pointing out its shortcomings. They take the second option and then – surprise, surprise – find it does not do the job properly. Who do they blame? No surprise here, it is you. And it is completely useless reminding them of your earlier reservations. They will respond by saying something like 'Well, if that was really your view you should have insisted.' And they have a point. Most businesses have their version of this sort of thing. At worst, not standing up to customers in this way means their perception of you changes, and next time they could place work elsewhere as a result.

The same principle applies with simpler things. An example can illustrate this. In a market research company one of the largest clients was causing the manager they dealt with considerable problems. The client's disorganization was at the root of the problem. They were forever cancelling or changing meetings and demanding attendance at others at short notice. They commonly telephoned demanding that the account manager rush to one of their many regional offices at a moment's notice. This sort of situation cost time and money, and ultimately threatened the viability of a carefully costed project. The instinct was to respond helpfully, to manage somehow to accommodate them. In this case, this just compounded the problem.

The client was of the 'give us an inch and we will take a mile and half' school (aren't they all, you may say). Every helpful act simply made them feel anything demanded would be responded to positively. Ultimately, if demands go up and up, something must be done. But it is a question of degree. Where do you draw the line? Perhaps the best answer is sooner rather than later, despite the instinct to help on each individual occasion and the real fear that saying no jeopardizes the client relationship.

Action

Most customers are reasonable, even if they sometimes act unreasonably. Prompted to think, they do, in fact, realize that they are not your only concern, that you have other responsibilities, indeed other commitments. Perhaps they would rate you less highly if you had only one client – them. If they value the relationship then they will expect others to do the same. So if you say 'No' and effectively point this out to them, they will not immediately believe they are being misused. Thus there is a good deal of difference between just saying you cannot meet at a particular time, and saying that you have a prior customer commitment. They would doubtless not want you to cancel a meeting with them at short notice, so why should they expect you to do just that to someone else?

Couple this approach with offering an alternative and it becomes even more acceptable:'I cannot... but I can arrange for one of my colleagues to attend/I could make the following day.' Your manner here can shape opinion and image; the job is to make them see a reasonable alternative, not to tell them they are unreasonable (though this may sometimes be a final option).

To return to the market research example, once the client was stood up to, the result was not an explosion. They were nonplussed for a moment but accepted an alternative, and later, having been met with such a response on a number of occasions, became gradually less unreasonable – and more profitable.

Catch the costs

Providing costs are clearly and comprehensively identified, then if customers ask for something additional it must be flagged as such at once. 'Of course I can schedule that if you feel it's necessary, but do you really want to increase costs in that way?' In such a case your response can vary – but always avoid allowing a customer to dilute profitability.

This is an area where – despite the need to be seen to 'go the extra mile' – business sense must sometimes outweigh instincts, either to be helpful or careful; or both.

And another idea...

Image is both fragile and volatile. Of course, your work and expertise create much of it. It can be enhanced in particular ways, for example by your ability to make a cracking presentation. But the general day-to-day communication between you and your customers also contributes significantly. Customers do not want to deal with a mouse. They expect expertise to be coupled with confidence – in a word, 'clout'. Saying 'No' somewhat more often might save you some inconvenience (or money). More important, standing up to people when appropriate might well improve your standing with them.

What is certain is that, as the saying has it, if you look like a doormat people will walk all over you.

Distribution – the right channel

The complexity of the various chains of distribution that exist in every industry (and that are more complex in some than others) needs attention at any time; in tough times this is particularly an area for review and action. There is clear possibility here to increase sales and reduce costs.

Consider what is called a market map, a device that charts the way a company gets its wares to market. The figure opposite gives a generic example using the publishing industry for illustration.

Any organization can create such a chart just by thinking through how their business works. If you do not have your own version of this, draw one up soon. You might be surprised how seeing things in this form clarifies the possibilities for you. Remember that the picture produced is volatile, and that changes occur because of external factors, and can also be made to occur. For example, in the publishing industry electronic retailing (such as Amazon) is a comparatively new approach. And if a company decides to put more emphasis on selling books direct through their own website, then this may need an additional channel to be added (see: www.koganpage.com for an example of this).

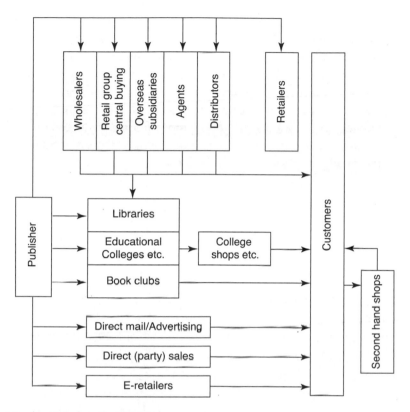

Market Map – Publishing

Action

Such a chart can act to remind marketing people that distribution is a marketing variable. That is, an organization can
decide which channels to work through, which to major on
and perhaps which to leave on the sidelines or ignore. Such
decisions must be predicated on the basis of fact, so an analysis of what proportion of business is flowing through the
different channels is necessary – hence an element of this
review involves adding in actual sales figures. Many of the

ways in which products and services are made available result from this sort of analysis, and the market map provides a very useful device for planning and implementing marketing strategies. An 'emergency' revisiting and updating of this principle might prompt a change of practice that helps in tough times, opening up a new channel, getting more from a neglected one or cutting back and saving resources being spent on another that produces poor results at high cost.

And another idea...

Talk to your financial colleagues; it may be that some permanent changes to your management control and accounting procedures can give you regular figures in a form that highlights how channels are working. Such information is all computerized these days and this is not too complicated. If you can see easily and regularly what is happening (and perhaps link to an analysis of trends), then fine-tuning of activity is possible more promptly and on every scale and that can, in turn, improve results.

21

Scrap marketing no-no's

Marketing can be simplistically described as activity to bring in the business. It needs to be done effectively yet is rarely said to be easy. Marketing activity must be customer-focused, continuously deployed, creatively originated and deployed and a complex mix of activity organized and co-ordinated to maximize effectiveness. It needs planning and a systematic approach, it needs... Enough. Surely there must be some straightforward approaches that work without great cost and effort when tough times put us under pressure?

There may well seem to be, but you must beware the danger of pursuing what appears to be a 'quick fix', something that is all too easy when budgets and time are under pressure.

Action

The action here is simply to avoid drifting into inappropriate 'easy' activity. Several approaches, chosen as the most common traps, can, in fact, cause problems and provide some examples.

All the following might be described as forms of 'ad hoc' marketing. Such include:

■ *Doing something only when there is time:* when workload permits, do some marketing. But marketing activity must fit not your timing, but that inherent in the market and with customers. Failing to maintain continuity can quickly lead to so called 'feast and famine': a situation with which many small firms are familiar. As a result, one minute there can be no prospects to follow up and convert, the next – after a burst of activity – there can be too many simultaneous leads to deal with properly.

■ *Convenient action:* activities favoured because of some particular factor that makes them convenient – Mary's got some free time this week, let's get her on the telephone to a few people. Mary may not be up to the job, and the telephone may not be the best form of contact.

■ *Subcontracting:* in other words, selecting marketing activity that you can get someone else to do. This seems easy, and is also easy to decide (everyone votes for something that will not involve them in any personal hassle). A quarterly newsletter that can be produced externally, perhaps by a public relations consultancy, is a good example. Many companies have got locked into producing such a thing, rejoiced that it is easy to do, then found that it does not produce good returns.

■ *Familiarity:* just because you may be good at something does not make it first choice for use. For example, a financial services firm stopped using cartoons on their promotional material after research showed that their clients viewed them as frivolous and inappropriate, much to the disappointment of the member of staff who loved drawing them

■ *On offer:* for example in advertising. One firm of printers recalled that almost all their promotional budget for the year had been spent when magazines telephoned them with offers of 'a special feature on promotional print and all your competitors are taking space'. Some of this was no doubt useful, but the ideal mix demanded more.

■ *What is fashionable:* this is a form of copycat action and as such is never to be recommended (of course you can copy or adapt methodology, but there should always be reason for it beyond simply viewing it as good 'because XYZ does it'), especially as an alternative to some original thinking.

■ *Perpetuating the same action:* sometimes a good idea continues in use beyond its usefulness, for no other reason than that it has become familiar and thus easy. Given a choice between more of the same and taking time to adapt or innovate, more of the same wins, and wins again, until method is stale and results confirm this. The antithesis of this can pay dividends. For example, should you reprint that brochure or rewrite it first?

■ *Action unsupported by appropriate skills:* if the personal skills that are involved are inadequate to the task then any good will be, at the least, diluted. For example, one of us (PF) recently attended the budget briefing of a local firm of accountants. Such events can work well and are well proven, but the poor standard of presentation (and lack of interest it sparked in the audience) negated any good effect. Similarly, a letter that PF recently received was individually written and personally addressed. It contained an apology (don't ask!) and made sales points for the future. But it was so strikingly old-fashioned and full of 'office speak' that it negated its message entirely.

■ *Panic action:* this is never a good idea. If sales drop or competition increases and urgent action is required, it is even more important than usual that action is thought through. Time spent in reconnaissance is seldom wasted. Ill-considered action, which might reflect others of the approaches listed here, is never likely to work as well.

Considered and co-ordinated

Marketing activity must not be skimped. It must surely be done properly or not done at all. That does not mean that nothing other than elaborate and expensive action will prove useful. The reverse may well be true. But action must be well considered. A great deal hangs on it, so it is surely worth some thought.

For most organizations the phrase 'marketing mix' is right. There is rarely one technique that works so well that others are unnecessary. A mix is needed. Consideration, not least of what works best in the market, must lead to sensible decisions about which mix is the current 'best buy' for you. Then activity must be deployed creatively – ideas are important to marketing, which continues to be as much an art as a science in tough times. And the various activities must be well co-ordinated to get the most from them. It is this co-ordination that can help maximize the simplest mix – where one thing builds on another, adding power and becoming a plan of action that is best for one simple reason – it does work and brings in the kind of business required, when it is wanted.

And another idea...

As a checklist to make sure that hard-pressed time, effort and money are not being wasted on ad hoc marketing, make sure marketing activity is:

- reflecting a focus on customer attitudes, preferences and needs;
- embodying a considered approach (preferably linked to a plan);
- providing continuity – rather than creating fits and starts;
- creative – ideas matter;
- well co-ordinated, so that different activities form a cohesive whole and act well together;
- regularly rethought, revised and updated.

22

Customer relationship management – encouraging loyalty

Even when times are good you will have the occasional situation where one of your customers gets upset about something. When you're going through a rough patch and business is hard to find, about the last thing you need is to lose a client.

Action

Should one of your consumers become angry about something, don't respond by losing your temper too. The first step in dealing with a dissatisfied customer is to find out the reason why they are upset. Is it your fault or one of your staff? Is it their fault?

The next thing you need to do is to listen. It's important to let the person vent their anger even if it is straight in your face. You must keep cool, and show that you are sympathetic to the situation. The consumer will (eventually) calm down.

Show concern by saying things like: 'How frustrating for you', 'I can see how infuriating that must be.'

Once the customer has expressed their feelings and realized that you are listening and understand their predicament, they will be (visibly) less upset. Anger is usually a short-term emotion. The key is allowing someone to explode. Until it is released their fury will accumulate and fester. Someone who is allowed a one-sided shouting match will be more co-operative later on. Listening and acknowledging the emotion they are experiencing will help them to calm down. You will have convinced them that you care.

It could be that you're the unfortunate recipient of some stored-up anger from other things that have nothing to do with the complaint you're trying to sort out. Don't – whatever else you may do – take it personally. The client will probably be eternally grateful to you for being allowed to get a lot of other things off their chest.

You must try to take back control of the situation once you've heard the person out. Tell your customer that you wish to help solve the problem and that you will do everything that you can within your responsibility to do so.

Focus on the issue and the possible solutions, not the emotions. If the consumer is abusive, repeat in a calm voice that you want to help. Explain that you can do this better if they tell you what they want. If appropriate, ask someone else to assist you, such as a colleague or your superior.

You can show interest by calling the person by name and letting them know that you are listening. Show empathy. Imagine if the boot were on the other foot. How would you react in a similar situation? To help you behave in an appropriate manner, draw on your own personal experiences of times when you have been confused, misunderstood or needed an answer or explanation.

Restate the essence of the complaint, clearly so that there are no misunderstandings between you and the injured party. Before taking any steps, make sure you understand the criticism, objection, request or need. Consider the possibility of human error. Perhaps the customer misheard something. Maybe the information they have been given is incorrect, or they may not have all the facts.

If there is a serious problem, admit it and apologize, at once. It is wise, as well as honest, to hold up your hands and accept your mistake (if it is something that you've done). Be open and say how sorry you are. Explain how it happened, for example that you should have put the order through manually but that you entirely forgot to do so. Apologize and express remorse that it has caused so much trouble.

This usually has the effect of taking the angry person entirely by surprise, because it is so rare for anyone to admit they've messed up and to take responsibility for working out a solution. You need to establish what sort of solution will appease the client. Offer alternative suggestions, not just one. But so long as you offer to put things right in a reasonable way that suits the customer, they are likely to end up feeling very satisfied indeed. Not only have you resolved the problem, you've also been honest with them.

The bonus here is that this course of action has the effect of reassuring the customer that they are dealing with a reputable organization, one that they can reasonably confidently continue to do business with. They will be well aware that everyone can make a mistake occasionally. At least you've had the guts to admit it, and put it right.

Make sure they realize that you are taking personal responsibility for sorting out the problem until it is resolved satisfactorily. Identify the timescale. If the problem cannot be rectified immediately, tell the customer how long it is likely to take – even if you fear this may involve a further outburst of indignation.

Summary

Ways to smooth a disgruntled customer's feelings:

- listen to their objection;
- repeat this back to ensure there is no misunderstanding;
- accept responsibility for sorting out the problem;
- inform them what steps you are going to take to rectify the situation;
- ask questions relevant to the issue;
- agree the next step towards reparation.

And another idea...

You may be advised by some people never to admit blame when dealing with customers in case they sue you. They may have a point. It would be wise to take legal advice if the situation is so serious that your mistake has cost them a really large amount of money. In the majority of cases a dissatisfied customer is not going to go to the trouble of suing your organization. It may have cost them some time or some money, but that's no big deal. As long as you are paying up, or recompensing them in some way, they should be satisfied. Lawyers may say that refusing to admit blame is probably the wisest course of action, but from a customer relations point of view, it is always better to admit it if you are wrong.

23

The art of saying no

Here's a specific way of dealing with the issue of time management when things are tough and everything is difficult at work and elsewhere. Forget about it. Do nothing.

Hold on, what does this mean? In one sense, time management is bad? No one should try to fill every second of every day with a task? Some people (those who seem bone idle to the rest of us hard-working types) seem to have got this down to a fine art already. But the overriding school of thought of results by volume is not necessarily the only way to go.

There is another way of looking at things. If you do what you've always done, you'll get what you've always got. So maybe, when (economically) times are tough and you are expected to achieve more with every minute spent in the workplace, you should be taking the opportunity to check out the other viewpoint? Why not try working hard at doing nothing like as much? Less can sometimes lead to so much more.

In case you're thinking this is heading in a rather strange direction for a book about action plans and survival strategies for difficult times, consider this. If you had nothing to do for a whole day, would you feel guilty? Are you comforted in some way by having so many demands on your time? Do you sometimes boast about the absurdly over-long hours that you spend working? When you're catching up with friends, do you vie with each other about who has had the earliest start in the morning? 'I was on the 05.40 train today. That's the third time this week.' Perhaps you'll recognize the character in the office (I hope it's not you) who rushes around, in their shirtsleeves, with their mobile phone pressed to their ear, showing everyone else what a busy bee they really are.

The point being made here is that being active is often a cover for avoiding critically important but uncomfortable actions. There are limitless options for creating 'busyness', particularly in the workplace environment. You can spend hours reorganizing your database or your e-mail address book. You could take a whole morning phoning people who really aren't interested in talking to you or listening to what you say – some people call this networking. Others spend the hours between 9 am and 5 pm walking about with a handful of papers. They are off to see someone, going to a meeting, just popping upstairs to accounts, heading towards the photocopier to duplicate documents they don't need. Perhaps it's time to check the BlackBerry again – after all, it's at least two minutes since you last looked to see what is, or isn't, happening on your mobile technology.

This list could go on and on. But the idea being aired is that if you are brave enough to stop being busy for a day you might actually increase your results more than you'd ever thought possible. Believe it or not, the way to accomplish more is by doing less. In fact, it's the only way to achieve it.

Action

So what's this great new idea? Elimination. Saying 'No'.

1. Try very hard – and this will be difficult at first – not to do something. Don't react just because someone says you should (or you think it's better to look busy rather than idle). How can you, if you're an employee for instance, actually free up your time? Let's take for example the fact that you spend between eight and ten

hours a day in your work place. Do you actually produce work all of that time? If you say yes, I don't believe you. It's not possible in a working environment for you to be productive for 100 per cent of the time.

2.   In which case, wouldn't it be better to negotiate with your employer (the self-employed here are already way ahead of the game) that you work one day a week from home? This would increase the amount of work you'd get done and have other knock-on effects. There's no doubt that you could achieve a normal day's output at the office in, say, a quarter of the time working uninterrupted from your home. Do you remember the last time you wrote up the minutes to a meeting in just over an hour in the quiet of your home, as compared with it taking almost the whole morning in the office? Now do you see what I'm getting at?

3.   Don't be confused by the difference between effectiveness and efficiency. Efficiency is performing a given task (whether important or not) in the most economical manner possible (stuffing envelopes can be done efficiently – if you have all the inserts laid out on the table and the envelopes are self-seal and you have a franking machine). But it's probably a required task rather than an important one.

4.   Effectiveness is doing the things that get you closer to achieving your goals. What's the point of being efficient in checking your emails twenty times a day? You may have developed an elaborate system of folders for storing them, with sophisticated retrieval techniques to locate these irrelevant communications once you've filed them. But why? What does this activity achieve?

5.   Remember this golden rule: doing something unimportant well does not make it important. If a task requires a lot of time to accomplish this does not make it important

either. What you do is infinitely more important than how you do it. Efficiency does matter, of course, but it is useless unless it is applied to the right things.

6. So find a day this week – that's all it takes. Put aside everything seemingly urgent and do some intensely hard work – spend time thinking.

7. Analyse what things are causing you problems and unhappiness. Work out what actions are resulting in desired outcomes and satisfaction. Apply these questions to everything from your business, finances, your customers, advertising, whatever you're involved with – even regarding your friends, your social life, your neighbourhood.

8. Don't expect this to be easy – you'll never have worked so hard in your life. Do you know what makes it so frightening? You're stepping out of your comfort zone – your straitjacket of your routine activities. But the idea is to identify your inefficiencies in order to eliminate them. Conversely, you should find your strengths so that you know what to multiply.

And another idea...

As a result of this change in your thinking pattern, you should be able to make several simple but far-reaching (emotional possibly) decisions that could change your life. Two examples: What about asking to relocate to another office within the organization? It wouldn't be a complete step into the unknown but it would be different. Or would it be possible to continue to work in the same sector/profession but as a freelance consultant rather than as an employee? You would have the freedom to work for yourself, and choose your hours. These questions might be hypothetical, but just think about it – what if?

24

Killing the problem before it kills you – stress busting

You may right now be working all hours in the day because times are tough and you've got to ensure that you provide as much help as possible. It's a known fact that working long hours increases stress levels. A result of your being stressed is that you work less effectively.

If you're working for someone else, spending your time doing pointless things, that isn't your problem, is it? Some people believe there is no incentive to use your time well, unless you work for yourself. So here's the double whammy – your stress levels increase because you're spending hours and hours working at futile things that other people want you to do and they don't seem to make any difference. Because your work doesn't achieve anything, you feel demoralized and get home stressed out. Why? Because what you've been doing all day hasn't made an iota of difference. The result? You wonder why you bothered. What better example of a downward spiral can you get?

Still feeling stressed, you stagger into work the next day. You are probably trapped in your office between the hours of 9 am and 5 pm, because that is the agreed time you go to work. During these hours people shuffle papers, generate unnecessary information and communicate unimportant and irrelevant things to each other by means of interminable and tedious meetings or lengthy telephone calls and e-mails. That's the way it is. After all, it's best to create activities so that people's working day is filled to capacity. Everyone knows time passes quicker if you're busy. Meanwhile, your blood pressure is rising and you're beginning to feel ill.

Action

1. When it comes to stress management – or perhaps stress elimination is the better description here – the key is to do something in the shortest amount of time possible and achieve a result.

2. If you have eight hours to fill during the working day, you will find things to do to fill those eight hours. But if you had 15 hours to fill, you'd fill all 15. Conversely, if there was an emergency and you needed to leave the office in two hours but had work to finish, somehow you'd manage to complete that work in two hours flat. How does this happen?

3. Perhaps you are familiar with Parkinson's Law? It sort of goes hand in hand – conversely – with the Pareto Principle (the 80/20 rule). The difference is that Parkinson's Law dictates that a task will swell in (perceived) importance and complexity in relation to the time available for its completion. Now do you understand?

4. So the magic formula for stress busting is – the imminent deadline. Simple isn't it? Sorted!

5. You have 24 hours to produce a detailed report and examination of the organization's performance over the last 12 months. It needs to be ready for a meeting with the shareholders which is tomorrow at 7 pm. Will you manage it? Yes, because you will be focusing on achieving the result.

6. The beauty of the short deadline is that you can only do the bare essentials. No time to waste on inconsequential things. If you had ten days to complete the task, think of the size of the mountain you could create out of this molehill. What if you had two months in which to do it? Don't even go there…

7. The bonus here is that invariably the end product of the shorter deadline is of equal or higher quality due to the greater focus on the result.

8. You achieve something of tangible benefit in a short amount of time. This permits only minimal stress build-up because of the relatively quick timescale. It is possible to be uncomfortable for a short amount of time because you know it will be over soon. If you don't know how long an unpleasant situation is going to last, it quickly becomes unbearable and stressful.

9. By the time you've got the piece of work completed, you're probably tired out. The adrenalin rush you experienced (healthy stress) to accomplish the task may be wearing off. You feel exhausted, but hey, what's this? The endorphins (hormones that give you a feeling of pleasure after exertion) are kicking in because you've satisfactorily achieved the required task within the time limits and the work is to a high standard.

10. Did you notice anything missing? No distress (unhealthy stress).

And another idea...

If you can manage it, the best solution is to work using the Pareto Principle (80/20 rule – 80 per cent is often good enough/20 per cent of effort produces 80 per cent of results) together with Parkinson's Law (shorten work time to limit tasks to the important ones). Identify the few critical tasks that contribute most towards getting job satisfaction and schedule them with very short, clear deadlines.

It's not enough knowing what the most important things are that you have to do, if you don't impose strict deadlines that create focus in order that you'll achieve them. Don't spend any more time getting stressed, jumping from one interruption and futile task to another. Start eliminating stress before it eliminates you.

25

Maximize business-winning skills

It should be clear that any business skill that links directly to winning business cannot be allowed to go by default during tough times. Take the example of making presentations. This is not everyone's forté, though most can learn to do a good job of it if they must.

Those presentations linked directly to winning business affect your profitability and likelihood of surviving in good shape when sales may be declining. Say you must make formal 'pitches' as a regular sales tactic to win business. Some people in the organization may be better at this than others. Let us say that, star performers apart, the percentage of presentations resulting in sales (this might be immediately or later depending on the kind of business involved) is 50 per cent. That might be fine in the good times; the ratio seems okay, sufficient business is coming in and it is easy to let matters ride.

As business buoyancy declines the number of opportunities for making presentations declines and so does the strike rate. What is coming in will soon be very much not enough. Attitudes change too: a presentation that resulted in business in good times may not now do so. Customers become more demanding and they equate a good presentation with professionalism; a lacklustre one no longer gives them sufficient confidence to place an order.

Even to stay in the same place conversion rates must increase from the old norm; to get ahead the quality of what is done must excel.

Action

Training is one budget that is always vulnerable to cuts in tough times. It pains us to say so (both authors undertake training) but there are areas of training that can wait. On the other hand, perhaps there are areas where tough times demand a training initiative; the case for training key staff in making effective presentations in the scenario described above is surely compelling. Perhaps it is invidious to put up with lacklustre performance in so important an area at any time, though it does happen. In tough times it may be tantamount to commercial suicide. Such training can bring immediate results, both from the learning that takes place and from the awareness that is generated of what must be done and why.

Training alone may be insufficient. Another common fault is that presentations are poorer than they should be, and indeed, can be, only because they are rushed. Insufficient preparation is done, justified by the – often mistaken – belief that someone can 'wing it'. If the whole process is taken more seriously, if management stresses the importance, demands that due preparation is done, that rehearsals take place where necessary (especially needed with team presentations) then standards and results can improve and do so quickly.

The same may be true in a number of areas, including the writing of sales proposals where exactly the same kind of issues apply as described here, and in other areas from computer skills to negotiation.

> Despite the tradition of quickly cutting the training budget when times become difficult, some training should become a priority and swift action can then have a significant positive effect.

And another idea...

Training is easily dismissed as a waste of money. Remember the old story of the manager saying, 'I'm not wasting money on training; what happens if people then leave?' To which the answer is simple: 'What happens if you don't train them – and they stay?' If you are still seeing training as a waste of money despite what has been said here, remember that training encompasses a great deal more than a formal course. Even reading this book can be regarded as low-cost training, and a host of different methodologies are available. Check them out, make sure they do the job (poor training is worse than none and just wastes money), but think hard before you simply wipe out training as an option.

26

Better abroad?

If markets are down at home, maybe you should go overseas. Of course launching into an export programme from scratch is a major development and perhaps not for tough times, given the level of time and investment it might demand. But some overseas initiatives may be sensible.

Action

Cross-border marketing and distribution seems to work best when it fulfils seven criteria:

1. *A strong corporate philosophy:* in other words, a strong brand image, corporate identity, style and culture – that travels.

2. *A genuinely new offering:* it may be radically different (like Tesco in Thailand) or more a matter of style, shopping experience or value, but it must exist – there is no right for every business concept to work everywhere no matter how closely it mirrors existing practice.

3. *Product acceptability:* the product must work in whatever market is considered.

4. *An appropriate format:* whether it is high-quality (like Gap), discounting (like Aldi), specialist sector focus (like Toys R Us), or high-end luxury (like brands such as Gucci).

5. *A clear target market:* often younger rather than older, affluent rather than further down-market seems most favoured.

6. *Commitment:* such global expansion needs to have weight behind it: money and perhaps especially dedicated people at senior level.

7. *A long-term view:* it may take time, and expecting or insisting on a rapid return may kill a project stone dead (eg IKEA was in the USA for eight years before it made a profit, yet their expansion has continued successfully).

Certainly international business brings increased risk, and a sound understanding of local markets (and therefore local knowledge) is important. In addition, an important area for many products when operating at a distance is service. This may mean a customer having the ability to get parts and repairs done on something like a camera or a radio, and get it fast, easily and effectively – especially so if anything is necessary during a warranty period. Another major difference between home-based operations and global ones for many organizations is simply the distances involved. A variety of types of organization may be involved, of course, but let us use the classic overseas distributor as an example. Without a doubt the level, quality and frequency of contact maintained is a significant direct influence on the success of the relationship and the level of revenue produced.

Such contact must:

- provide information (sound, useful and timely);
- be motivational (to people ranging from the distributor's principal to their sales and service staff);

■ genuinely help to improve business performance (thus making the relationship work, promoting loyalty and helping increase sales).

The genuine help provided can involve a number of different things, including assistance for the distributor with:

■ planning;
■ finances and financing;
■ training;
■ staff maintenance and motivation;
■ industry and competitive intelligence;
■ technical innovation;
■ public relations and image;
■ standards and controls;
■ business efficiency and improvement of effectiveness.

As part of an overall review of opportunities and prospects, it is worth considering just what embryo overseas business can be accessed.

And another idea...

The IT revolution has provided a new way to implement a global channel of distribution – without leaving your desk. E-tailing apart, large numbers of organizations now have websites. This may lead the way into international distribution, it may go in parallel with other channels, or provide a way of stimulating orders from a market where no other activity is undertaken, but almost certainly it complicates matters.

Setting up this sort of facility seems easy, but of course it must be done well. People must recognise the product and be aware of the route to information and purchase before they can, or will, act. Many people access websites but then give up on them because they are confusing or badly organized. In addition, setting up the facility is one thing, leading people to it and prompting its use is quite another. So, while e-commerce provides seemingly instant access to all the markets of the world at once, the facts suggest that concentrating on supplying specific markets through their own local channels has merit too.

Whatever you do overseas, any (profitable) business it creates can fill a hole when home sales are dropping. It may be an important development for the business in the long term too.

27

Saving your skin by saving your work – computer backup

There used to be two certainties in life – death and taxes. Now there are three – death, taxes and the inevitability that your computer system will go down and you'll lose all your precious data if you haven't backed it up.

There's no doubt about it, computers are fantastic. That is, until they inexplicably stop working. When that happens things are not quite so jolly (trust us – as writers we've been there). What you need, of course, is some form of insurance. Bear with us here – the point is not whether you know about backing up, it is whether everything necessary is, in fact, being done. There is no worse time to hit a problem than when times are tough (and the problem could have been avoided).

During difficult times, you need to keep an eye on the bottom line. You are naturally concerned with saving costs and not wasting money. But the real bottom line is that you can't manage without your IT system. It doesn't matter whether your organization is minute (one person – ie you) or huge (we're talking world domination league here), no business can manage without computers. Just think for a moment how much work is generated all over the globe, every day, every hour, every minute, every second on these machines. Computers enable vast amounts of work to be produced quickly, information processed at the press of a button, and presented professionally. But for some unknown reason of mechanical, electrical or alien force, all your work can suddenly disappear without a trace. Frighteningly, it is usually irrecoverable.

The professional (and personal) data on your hard drive is, without doubt, the most important and valuable thing inside your computer. Scary as this thought is, it is the only part of your computer that cannot be replaced. It may be irritating and sometimes expensive replacing a failed memory chip, or even a processor, but there is no replacing data once it is lost. This is why you must set up – at the earliest possible opportunity if you haven't already done so – a back-up system.

Simple hard drive failure may be the most common cause of data loss; however, the threat of smart Internet worms and viruses has become an increasing cause of data loss or corruption. Although it is impossible to provide absolute guaranteed protection for your hard drive, there are a number of different ways that you can minimize the risk of losing all your important data by making regular backups of your information.

Action

There is probably no solution that is one hundred per cent safe and solutions (like everything to do with IT) date as you watch, but check out the possibilities of having a back-up in whatever form – ideally of your whole computer (something that currently implies a separate hard disk back-up) – update it regularly and keep it safe and separate from the original.

And another idea...

Paranoia is the highest level of data security. If you are a small nation state or a global organization, you will have all of your data running simultaneously on two totally separate systems – side by side. This means in separate locations, operated by separate manufacturers. This is the ultimate belt and braces approach to backing up your irreplaceable data. In some countries huge amounts of money are spent on new computer systems and, no doubt, back-up facilities which (when unveiled) proceed not to work – even on the best of days.

Not a bad business to be in – IT consultant, computer backup organization or system designer. You get paid whether the system works or not and you certainly don't need to be understood by your customers...

28

Learning from experience – knowing your customers

One of the most effective ways of keeping the bottom line (or possibly even increasing it) during tough business times is to extend the relationship-building process with your existing customers. How? By simply enquiring and listening. I'm referring of course to a customer satisfaction survey.

Customer feedback means getting to know what your customers think about you and your organization. For any organization it can prove a remarkably effective and inexpensive source of market research. In a tough economic climate it makes total sense to take action – you have nothing to lose and much to gain.

These are some of the things you can find out:

- who your customers are;
- if they're not your customers but you thought they were, when they are likely to be your customers;
- why they are your customers and not someone else's;
- what your customers want;
- how your customers feel;

- what your customers think;
- how you can make your customers feel valued;
- what sort of initiatives your customers would appreciate;
- what you can do to keep your customers loyal;
- how you can give yourself a competitive edge over others.

There is a huge amount of information here, and once gathered it can be used by the management structure to drive the organization forward in the right way, according to current market trends.

Action

Formulate your own questionnaire. You may not need to ask your customers all the questions listed above but you should take the trouble during a survey like this to find out as much as you can about their psychology. What's important here is that you are taking the time to talk to people who already do business with you, or are planning to do so. Many of them have already paid money for your services, and may be flattered that you value their opinion. They are less likely to desert you in times of difficulty if you have made them feel important and valued.

Before embarking on such a survey, you should review existing information or research data concerning customers and customer satisfaction. You should find out:

- what you know about your existing customers;
- what you know about their expectations;
- how well you are meeting those expectations;
- what will happen in the future to customer requirements;
- how you compare to your competitors;
- how the market is likely to change in the next one to three years.

Let's imagine a customer satisfaction survey being carried out by a professional service organization that re-branded three years before. They want to find out whether the new image has changed the perception of the business generally. The management conducts a survey by interviewing 50 companies made up of existing customers, potential customers and market influencers.

They design a simple questionnaire (as detailed above), and include a mix of closed and open-ended questions to capture opinions and perceptions. They invite customers (this can be by letter or a telephone conversation) to score the company on image, identity, reputation and its provision of services. In addition they ask their customers about the company's relative strengths and weaknesses, and where the customers see opportunities for the organization's future growth.

A survey such as this will help any organization to update its business strategy for the future, based around its existing customer base. It will influence how it can compete even more successfully with its known competitors.

Successful outcome

One customer satisfaction survey (carried out by the writer, hired as consultant researcher to an organization of architects) was hugely beneficial. The results showed that the organization was professional and those surveyed had confidence in its ability to deliver its services well. They found the management and staff approachable and competent in handling any difficulties that arose, but it was evident from the survey that the organization's contact database needed updating.

And another idea...

Within six months this architectural practice had won a significant number of new projects. The survey results were tangible. Within a year the annual turnover had increased by 19 per cent.

This is something that you can do within your own business – and you can do it now. You really can't afford not to. New business is most likely out there, waiting for you, just for the asking.

29

Spotting new opportunities – strategic alliances

Now times are tough, are you searching for new ways to grow your business? Do you actively seek ideas that will positively impact on your bottom line? Have you thought of making friends with the enemy? It's easy to overlook the competition as a resource, but all you have to do is look at things in a different way. If you shift your focus to view your competitors as an addition to your supply chain rather than a rival to it, you will discover opportunities that would otherwise remain unknown to you.

Thinking of competitors as allies rather than opponents is not new. Strategic alliances are often the way forward for small to medium sized organizations. Co-operation with competitors, customers, suppliers and companies producing complementary products can expand markets and lead to the formation of new business relationships. In some cases it can create new forms of enterprise.

Co-operation in difficult times makes more sense than competition. The idea of teaming up with competitors to develop new ideas and to make your organization better at what is does, delivers a challenge to many people. But there are a number of ways of doing this. Strategic alliances can be formal and encompass only a specific project. At other times they are informative and active with only certain types of projects.

Action

1. *Development or extension of products or services:* if your business is customer-focused, you will actively seek out the best ideas and ways of serving your customers' needs. But combined strengths can produce amazing results. By collaborating with a competitor you might be able to win new contracts neither of you could do alone. One plus one can often equal much more than two.

2. *Apportioning referrals:* consider having at least three people or companies to whom you would refer business without hesitation. Ideally there should be a mutual understanding that the favour will be returned. Whether you have arranged a referral fee, a reciprocal referral, or you are the one that wins the project, everyone is a winner.

3. *Get in the know:* it is essential to find out which are the best organizations producing complementary or related services in your own market. Knowledge is power and if your customers perceive you as the place to go for information, your business reputation will grow. Your customers will value your intelligence and connections in the market.

4. *Best practice:* you can learn something from everyone and every situation. No one can possibly have all the answers, which is why sharing best practice is so important. It does not mean sharing trade secrets or colluding on fees. What it means is coming together for improvement. True

professionals subscribe to the principle of abundance and see the power of helping each other to get better. 'A rising tide lifts all boats.'

5. *Risk awareness:* it is important to bear in mind the possible pitfalls when contemplating strategic alliances with a competitor, or anyone else. One possible issue is the lack of common goals amongst the parties. If the collaboration does not work, perhaps the synergies were not real or the communication system was flawed. It is wise to do some research before committing yourself to such an alliance – a corporate version of the pre-nuptial agreement.

And another idea...

The obvious benefits of strategic alliances mostly outweigh the risks. But it is essential to pay attention to whether you really can work together. Complementary areas of expertise are one thing, but do the personality types fit together? The question to ask is, 'Can these people really add value to the project/product/service?'

The ability to create successful strategic alliances is a valuable skill to acquire. You need to have total awareness of your own company's strengths and weaknesses, as well as that of your potential ally. Look for complementary abilities. Your ideal partner is a business that enhances what you do.

30

Detox and save (expenses)

This is a topic that applies both professionally and personally. If you can cut down, simplify and eliminate waste, you will be happier, healthier and better off. As I said, this could apply to someone's personal life – like turning your back on the cream cakes and packets of crisps, eating more fruit and healthy food, and going for a walk instead of popping into the pub.

You can apply these rules of cutting down or cutting out to business expenses when times are tough, and the results could be noticeable very quickly. You only need to take small opportunities to reduce expenditure and big savings will follow. An example could be your colleague who brings a lunchbox to work each morning. Do you admire this person or think they are an idiot because they get up ten minutes earlier than they need to, to make a sandwich and a smoothie? Perhaps you look down on them because they never go in the coffee shop across the road, which makes such excellent and mouth-watering take-away snacks.

But think about it from a financial point of view – if you spend £3 a day on buying yourself lunch, and you multiply that by the number of working days there are in a year (233 isn't it?), that's about £700 of your money – maybe even £1,000 of pretax income you're spending that your workmate isn't. If you want to feel even worse, £1,000 is about 4 per cent of an average annual salary in the UK (just on eating lunch).

It could be argued that some small businesses fail not because they make some gigantic error about market forces or bring out a product that no one wants or even invest badly. There is evidence that small items of expenditure, the ones you hardly notice, are responsible for sapping life-blood from some companies' bank balances. We're talking here about printer cartridges, phone bills, postages, taxi fares, etc. The smaller the items, the less likely they are to be flagged up on the organization's financial radar.

Here are a few suggestions for reducing your organization's outgoings before you have to cut and run.

Action

1. Take small steps to reduce expenditure and big savings will follow. But it might be an idea to set a target figure that you wish to have reduced expenditure by within, say, six months. You don't have to sack half your workforce immediately, return your organization's car or move to a rat-infested garret.

2. Review the number of subscriptions you pay to trade associations, clubs and other organizations. There may be some (paid by direct debit) that you don't even realize you're paying for, let alone get any value from them.

3. Do you receive lots of business and professional journals? These may be paid by annual subscription in advance. Check how many of them are relevant to the operation of your organization. Does anyone, you included, ever read them? See if you can reduce the number.

4. Have a look at, or get someone else to do so if appropriate, the telecom contracts you are paying for. There are so many deals around these days, unless you know a lot about it or have time to do the research, you may be paying well over the odds for the services you need. Great savings could be made here.

5. Don't upgrade the mobile phones or laptop computers just because a newer, more exciting version has come on the market. See what's out there, but be aware that prices for IT equipment often fall dramatically once a product isn't quite so state-of-the-art.

6. Send round a memo to all staff asking them to avoid dialling 0870 numbers. By using an alternative number (usually provided as the 'calls from overseas') simply replace the '+44' with '0' and you will not be paying premium rate for these calls.

7. Find the best deals from suppliers of stationery, light bulbs, paper towels, coffee/tea and other beverages, water dispensers, etc. In tough times, it pays to negotiate.

8. Organize a review of the spending on business credit cards. Even a clamp down on the limit that can be spent on client hospitality (unless it has been approved higher up the organization's structure) could make serious budget savings.

9. Reduce your corporate entertaining. Spend less time with big-spending business associates. It will prevent you from being profligate with hard-earned profits. Stick with the more modest types, or, if you can't avoid the flash mob, leave the restaurant early.

10. Does everything you put in the mail have to go first class? Postage costs continually increase, so it may be possible to send some letters second class and save money.

And another idea...

Detox. It would be a major decision to re-locate your offices to a less expensive area in order to save money but there is a simple idea you could put into practice. Maybe there is an empty room in your offices that has become a dumping ground for junk. If you detoxed/de-cluttered it would be space available to rent to a micro-business/sole practitioner. Of course you must check the terms of the lease and/or consult your landlord for their permission, if you don't own the premises. But it could prove a useful additional amount of income.

31

Listen carefully – information vs secrecy

Too little or too much? Do you suffer from information overload in your organization, or is it a miracle that anyone knows anything at all about what is going on? Are your managers experts at being 'economical with the *actualité*' (to paraphrase the UK politician, the late Alan Clarke)?

Information, we are told, is power. That is why some managers use information (or the withholding of information) to make sure that they are the most knowledgeable – and therefore the most important – individual in the organization.

But sometimes you have to be the bearer of bad news. There is an expression about 'shooting the messenger'. Perhaps it would be better to keep quiet and say nothing? But more often than not the truth (or a loose version of it) will out eventually. If in the meantime the workforce start gossiping and a lot of hearsay and half-truths abound, the cumulative result is a damaging one for all concerned.

Action

1. When things are tough business-wise (maybe there is the possibility of some workers being made redundant, or

organization budgets have been cut drastically and there's no money to take on extra staff so that orders can be delivered on time) it is better to bite the bullet and break the bad news. But do it as gently and positively as possible. The sooner this is done the better.

2. As long as you bear in mind that morale is likely to be seriously damaged, temporarily, you should try to get the message across as quickly and sensitively as possible. Once you have done that you can start the process of rebuilding confidence straight away. Try to be as positive as possible – but not to the extreme of cracking jokes and trying to make people laugh at what is obviously something very serious.

3. Tell the staff the reasons why the decision has been made. If you didn't make the decision, say so. Also, if you don't know who did, find out whose decision it was and make sure your information is correct. Doubts and ambiguities only make matters worse.

4. Remind your team/department what the goals and objectives are and reassure them that these can still be met. If for some reason (such as the decision that has just been taken) these objectives can't be met, re-adjust the targets so that they are achievable.

5. Let them know how sorry you are about how things have worked out. If compensation is an option, tell them what it is. Maybe you won't be increasing their salaries this year but you can allow them to go home an hour earlier on Friday afternoons.

6. For a morale boost, try to give them something they can put their energy in to. If they are good at organizing events, offer them the opportunity to raise funds for their pet charity – doing a fun run or similar.

7. If the bad news you have to communicate is that you have had to sack one of their colleagues, you must do so

immediately after the dismissed person has left the building.

8.   No confidential information must be given out about their ex-colleague's behaviour. You can tell them that you are sorry it has happened and that there was nothing personal in the decision. Explain that the dismissed person was preventing the whole of the team/department from achieving its full potential. It is quite likely that some of the staff were well aware of this and will understand.

9.   Tell them that you are confident that the department can now go forward and will be more successful as a result of the individual's departure. Explain that the decision to dismiss the member of staff was taken in the interests of the whole team.

And another idea...

Let's face it – some people are just bad communicators. They shy away from situations where they have to talk to people. Perhaps they are frightened of interacting with staff, or they 'forget' to tell their employees something. Perhaps they are just too busy. If you have someone in your organization who simply doesn't make the effort to communicate information on a 'need to know' basis, they are storing up trouble for themselves and the organization as a whole.

Whatever the reason for the communication failure, it contributes to an unhealthy corporate climate. This is particularly true when times are tough for many businesses. Staff need to be empowered with information so that they can make the best decisions at their own level in the organization. It is totally demoralizing if they cannot do anything without seeking the approval of those higher up the 'food chain'.

32

Fine-tune sales techniques

Selling is never easy, and in tough times it can be damned difficult. Imagine: this is just what you want – you are in front of a buyer, a good prospect, and have the opportunity to tell them about your product. You have ten minutes. Go!

Whoever is in this position in your organization it must be certain that the opportunity is maximized. Consider again: are you sure that ten minutes later what you will have said will have maximized your chances of coming away with an order? Honestly? And would it be any more likely if you had twenty minutes or half an hour? Of course, you know your product and can, doubtless, talk about it forever, but time is not on your side in selling. Buyers are busy and even if they do not impose a deadline, they may well have one in mind – or simply begin to glaze over after a while. In tough times sales methods that might scrape through and bring results in better times are just not enough.

Action

A review may be necessary to ensure that sales techniques exist, are up to date and are being deployed in a way that truly differentiates. Reviewing all sales techniques is beyond our brief, but the following may prompt some ideas. Let us assume there is a need, a possibility of selling despite any market problems (and questioning to identify customer needs is an important stage in the sales process) – what next? Various things help, not least a degree of logic, utter clarity and powerful description; but something else is important, indeed this perhaps comes first. There is considerable merit in ensuring that you can encapsulate your proposition succinctly, and in organizing the message so that it works well for the customer.

Organizing for success

Not only does it sometimes take too long to make a sales case, there is also another mistake. It is one that conditions the whole process. It is introspective. The seller begins – we are... we have... we do... and the litany continues far too long in this vein; all about them, nothing about the customer. Indeed, regularly this kind of content becomes two-thirds or more of everything that is said. Yet, surely customers want to know what is in it for them? Without a focus on that, the mental response tends to be one of 'So what?' At worst, people switch off or begin actively to look for the snags. Besides, in tough times if you do not have the courage of your convictions, why should anyone buy?

Again assuming they are potential customers and have a need for the product, people want to know three things above all. They ask if what is being put to them is:

▓ affordable and value for money – would they be prepared to pay for the advantages being spelled out?
▓ credible – do they really believe that what is offered is deliverable?

▓ competitive – is it the best deal if they are looking at several potential suppliers (which in tough times is more likely than ever)?

That being so, it makes a certain sequence logical in selling. First, they do want to know something about you. But this does not help them decide whether what you are selling is right for them or not, rather it helps create a platform from which to sell, setting out your credentials to be taken seriously. As such it is a short preliminary, not the whole case. Perhaps it is because this is the bit we know best, or feel safest discussing, that it so often takes over and pushes out other things that need to be said. Whatever the reason for that, this element of the pitch needs to be kept succinct.

Second, you need to get quickly to the crux of your case and tell people why they should buy from you. To begin to organize this in your mind you should just set out the reasons. Ask yourself – why should people buy? Make a list. Then ensure two things, that:

▓ all the points you make are benefits, not features (this is another issue but, for the record, benefits are what your product or service does for or means to the buyer, whereas features are simply factual things about it);

▓ the case is encapsulated in perhaps four to six points. This may mean combining some points together and leaving others out, perhaps for brief mention later. The reason for this is that some reasons are likely to be more powerful than others – so select these (and perhaps match them to particular prospects) – and that you are working against the clock. Too few may sound weak. You are seeking a number of points here that are sufficient to impress, yet remain manageable.

How do you do this? Start by asking yourself some questions about the effect buying from you has on your customers. For example, do you sell something that:

- helps them better control their business?
- improves their effectiveness or efficiency?
- reduces their operating costs?
- increases their productivity?
- introduces new approaches?
- improves quality?
- helps them create a competitive advantage?
- strengthens their customer service?

Go through every possible effect, then ask how this effect is generated and make sure that each is stated as a benefit. It is easy to state things from an essentially internal viewpoint: we have a list of blue chip customers. Impressive? Perhaps, but the point here is one of confidence: a new customer can feel there is safety in numbers, and will be impressed that well-known companies have checked you out and then found satisfaction with what is on offer. The benefits are safety and certainty, and maybe a saving of time. Prioritize your list to create the manageable core points you need.

So far so good

This sequence does three things. It begins to differentiate you from those who talk endlessly about themselves because you are quickly on to what is in it for your customer. It sparks interest early on and prompts people to adopt a positive approach to what comes next. Instead of saying 'So what?' they are more likely to become interested and begin to seek for a match with their own situation as they continue to listen. They already want to know more. You can check this with them as you go – 'If that seems of interest, let me spell out how it works.'

Building the case

Now a brief overview of key benefits will not, of itself, guarantee success. Rather, it sets the scene for what comes next. Now you can spell out the detail, revisiting the main points on the basis that these are of interest. You can show what makes them possible and create credibility so that people really believe that this is what they will get.

Your descriptions must be clear, memorable and matched to the buyer's situation – 'So you will find...' rather than 'We do this...'. Here you justify your case, add detail and build credibility – adding, as necessary, everything from facts and figures to testimonials.

Remember that no one buys anything unless they understand the case being put for it and (the most important factor) unless they really believe it. Successful selling must help people to buy, going about it in a way that matches how they make decisions, and creating belief as it does so.

Gaining a commitment

All the foregoing makes it seem something of a one-way process, which of course it is not. It is a conversation. This way, however, you have mentioned sufficient information – key reasons to buy – up front before the two-way conversation starts. You will catch their attention and persuade them that you are worth listening to, and you will do this early on.

As you continue they may well want to add comment and ask questions – even raise objections. Indeed you want them involved and there is merit in encouraging this. Then by the time you get to the conclusion – having made a powerful case, but not told them everything there is to say about your product – they too are at the point where a decision can be made. You need to close – ask for an order – and will have a good chance of getting one.

Realistically, there are other stages – the buyer insists on thinking about it, has to check with someone else or wait for a particular moment such as the start of a new budgetary period. But techniques can be applied to these situations too, aiming to get over problems and maximize your strike rate.

Structured to deliver success

What is being commended here is an antidote to a miscellany of points about what you offer, delivered in a long burst of enthusiastic introspection. You need to think through the logical order in which to lay out your case, based more on the way customers buy and on their thinking than on your own thoughts and convenience. The route described above, is designed to grab attention early on, get and keep people paying attention and do so in a constructive way – so they quickly believe that what is coming next should be worth hearing.

And another idea...

Above all, by establishing a core list of benefits and spelling out how these can be delivered, you adopt an approach that stands the greatest chance of establishing belief. More sales meetings probably fail to secure an order for lack of real belief than for any other reason – something seems a pretty good case, but people are just not quite sure. Without forgetting that there are other important sales techniques, an approach that allows your case to be presented in a way, and through a sequence, that builds belief is the surest way to sales success. If the detail of what is done all contributes to that you will be well on the way to bucking any sales decline.

33

Less is more

There are always good reasons to preserve the product line, and a fear that customers will cease to buy from you if you drop their favourite item. Usually these fears are overblown, but still rationalization is often delayed – avoided might be a better word. Management opt to 'look at it next year' or simply sideline any decision.

In tough times the drain an underperforming product can cause should not be ignored. It may be inherently less profitable than other products; indeed avoiding increasing their price 'in case we sell even less of them' is coupled with avoiding cutting poor performing products. Keeping it in the range may take up more time and incur more cost in stock holding for long periods and more.

And what about customers?

A similar situation may exist with certain small customers. Yes, there are some customers that you are better off without, and they may be both small and disproportionately troublesome, paying late or wanting special (and costly) attention, especially if they have dealt with you for a long time.

Usually in both cases the negative reaction to change is predicted to be more than it is if action is finally taken. If understanding is to be generated about such cuts then surely it is more

likely when tough times mean many things are being reviewed –
the logic is inescapable.

Action

So, both these areas should be addressed decisively. Several
stages are necessary:

■ First analyse the situation. You need to check the figures
to be sure that the financial case is as you suspect; indeed,
often it is worse than expected.

■ Make arrangements for any alternative action that may be
needed once a cut is made. For example, you may aim to
cease supplying a small customer but want to make
arrangements so that they can still order. This might
mean directing them to a wholesaler or website or
arranging to take telephone orders rather than having a
sales representative call on them. The job is to make
savings, but not to throw the baby out with the bath-
water, so you must make the alternative seem attractive.

■ Set a sensible timetable; you may need to act swiftly but
too precipitative action may cause problems.

■ Make sure that well-expressed advance notice is given to
customers and staff.

And another idea...

The cost savings here may be worthwhile, but time is also likely to
be saved. It is useful to actually match this with some new action. By
stopping doing something that is helping your situation little or not
at all, you have time to focus on something else that is more important and which will make a positive difference. Make sure you know
what that is and that it works; it is easy to find that time cleared in
this way just disappears amidst the general chores.

34

'Best buy' promotional mix

Cut advertising and what happens? Well for a while perhaps very little may change. The impact of what has been done in the past has a continuing effect and sales come in much as usual. One major company – the makers of Oxo – once experimented by curtailing all of their advertising to see what would happen. After a spell when little difference was seen, sales started to drop. New advertising was in the pipeline and was introduced before any further drop occurred, but it looked as if the next decline would be worse and occur more quickly.

So it would be for most businesses, but the gut reaction to tough times is to cut promotional budgets. The effect can be to make a bad situation worse. If sales are already down, then a lack of advertising can send them into a steeper decline.

The promotional mix will vary for each individual organization. It may include advertising, but also public relations activity, direct mail, sales promotion and a wealth of activities from exhibiting at a trade show to conducting promotional events.

If the response to tough times should not be to cut indiscriminately, then what should it be?

Action

Certainly promotion in all its forms needs to be assessed. Cuts may be possible and some activity may have been introduced for not very good reasons. But the rest needs to be assessed and may need to be focused differently. For example, if an organization markets to a range of segments, you need to be sure that it's worth targeting them all (the market map concept referred to on page 76 may be relevant here).

Check that:

■ all promotion matches chosen areas of the market (which might be a narrower range of potential customers than in better times);

■ messages are up to date and creatively presented;

■ timing is right across all activities (it is surprisingly common to see an advertisement and find that, say, a new product is not yet stocked – or even heard of – by retailers);

■ if you sell through complex channels, promotion to whatever middlemen are involved is important too; for example booksellers as well as readers must be made aware of a book, and many others may be involved too (as the market map chart on page 77 made clear).

And another idea...

For many businesses, perhaps especially smaller ones, tough times mean finding lots of different things to do to ring the changes and draw attention to your offering. A sign seen outside a travel agent flagging a one-off Sunday opening is a simple example of this (and hopefully the announcement was coupled with some public relations or promotional activity to make sure that more people came in on the day).

A simple way of tracking such activity is with a calendar/planning chart. This allows the whole period ahead to be seen as one spread and quickly identifies gaps where nothing is scheduled and more needs to be done.

35

Getting a little help from your friends (networking)

Tough times in business require tough decisions. So why don't you get on the phone to your friends? That may sound a little trite when you are facing a rough patch at work. But if a spoonful of sugar helps you swallow nasty tasting medicine, phoning a friend can help when the chips are down.

Who do you know well enough to ask for support when you need it? In other words, who is in your inner circle? How often do you see/speak to them? Is it only when you want something? When problems occur and you're looking for solutions? I hope not – because what you need now is your 'A team'.

Action

Call for reinforcements

The first people you should naturally want to speak to when you're 'stuck' on a problem or issue are those who you know will help. By speaking to one or two of them and asking 'What would you do?', 'Have you ever come up against this?' 'Who would you advise I talk to?' you should get a quick injection of common sense, practical advice or radical solution to what you may have thought was an insuperable problem.

Most people's inner circle consists of between five and ten people. They are people you know extremely well, with whom you've been friends for years. You have respect for them, they respect you. They may be people within your organization, or from another aspect of your life – from school days, university, wider family members, former colleagues or friends.

Asking advice

The whole point about your inner circle is that you would be prepared to do for them what they are prepared to do for you.

- You're sincerely interested in them and what they are doing.

- You know their likes and dislikes and genuinely care about their success and happiness.

- Whatever it takes, you keep in regular contact.

- You're alert to opportunities for introducing them to useful/influential people.

- You send regular, informative emails or meet up for informal updates.

You don't go to them just when there's a problem. You keep your visibility high, letting them know what you are doing, and asking about new developments in their life.

Shared standards

The relationship you've developed with them is because you share the same sense of values:

- honesty;
- sincerity;
- responsiveness;
- confidence;
- modesty;
- trustworthy;
- appreciativeness.

Your inner circle is your personal SAS. They are the rapid reaction force because their help and advice is almost instant. Networking at this level is a perfect mechanism but it will only develop over time (we're talking years). The principle is 'giving to receive'.

And another idea...

Make it a rule – however much you need them – when beginning the conversation to ask how they are and whether it is convenient to speak. (They may want to help you, but not if they're just driving to the hospital with their wife who is about to give birth.) When they ask you how they can help, tell them the truth. Don't be afraid to be honest and direct with your inner circle. These people are not fair-weather friends. Someone who knows you and your business this closely is going to want to support you. It's all about relationships, trust and respect.

36

Don't be cautious – be bold

As the economic climate worsens there is inevitably an increasing emphasis on competitiveness. The true value of ICT (information and communications technologies) is that it enables you to compete better. ITC also enables you to operate at a higher level of efficiency and profit.

Understanding the roots of competitiveness is the key to growth and success in difficult times. The issue that faces everyone is how to distinguish what will really make a difference (faced with so much data, unsolicited advice and competing marketing messages).

In the current climate your ICT must be used to:

1. Help generate more income.
2. Stop money spilling out.
3. Help achieve better performance from your people.
4. Make better use of physical resources.
5. Improve productive processes.
6. Improve money management.
7. Help deliver strong intangibles.

Action

1. *Help generate income:* tools for better product/production design; market research; market analysis; sales administration; account management; prospect tracking; call centre operation, market communication.

2. *Stop money spilling out:* financial and operational reporting; managing overheads; expenses policy and administration; time costs; asset management; budgeting; control systems.

3. *Better performance from people:* knowledge sharing and acquisition; communication tools and processes; skills and other training; presentation aids; time management.

4. *Better use of physical resources:* deployment; maintenance; replacement scheduling; purchasing; inspection; measurement; improvement programmes.

5. *Improve productive processes:* scheduling; capacity planning; logistics and distribution; back-up; monitoring; change management; project management.

6. *Improve money management:* product/service performance; warranty; billing efficiency; time period efficiency; investments; purchasing efficiency.

7. *Help deliver strong intangibles:* customer relations; perception of quality and value; communication; goodwill; brand recognition and equity; values; integrity.

Whatever your business does, you should be able to slot in to a number of the above areas. In all probability you will be able to deliver against this model in more ways than one.

And another idea...

As the saying goes, 'Nobody's perfect, but a team can be.' Ask your team if they can suggest ways in which this model can be improved or enhanced. (If you're feeling insecure about asking this question, imagine how they feel.) Allowing your staff to help generate a measurably greater competitive edge is the strongest position you could put yourself in at the current time. Don't miss your chance.

37

Pricing policy to maximize profitability

This section could just say, 'Times are tough, cut prices.' Certainly that is a gut reaction amongst many, but it can lead to a wholesale reduction in profitability, which will help not at all. So let's consider price positively.

First, let us put things in perspective. Price is part of your offering and for many people the strategy should be to link it firmly to quality and make a virtue of it. Would you regard a Rolls Royce in the same way if it cost the same as a Ford Ka? Unlikely. Think of the people who have recently regretted not spending more on insurance as they have bailed their houses out after the recent floods. Price and value for money go together.

Price and quality going together is normal. For the most part, people do not want the cheapest thing available. Walk round any supermarket and you will notice that the brand leaders are never the cheapest products. Consider why this is. Apart from a company's need to make profits, they need a margin that allows a higher price strategy to work. If you price too low you do not just lose profitability, you lose the ability to market effectively. Good marketing persuades people that quality is worth paying for and higher prices pay for good marketing. So the principle is sound, but you need to work out the right way to make it work.

A suitable position

Think where you want to be in the market. Most companies face a range of competitors, some offer less costly products and services, some more expensive. Do you want to be average or can you go for being amongst the more expensive? You may need to take a bullish view. And later you need to make sure you do not become inadvertently repositioned because you do not increase prices. It is, in any case, much easier to increase prices regularly than to leave it two or three years, as the larger increase that is then necessary always brings adverse comment, and in tough times can have customers voting with their feet.

There must be an appropriate match between product and price and, in turn, with image and service. Remember that the psychology of price is important here and that exactly how price is presented makes a difference to its acceptability. For example:

- Avoid round figures: people seem to buy more when price is set just below round figures – £9.99 seems less than £10.00. Similarly, £975 seems significantly less than £1,000. Do not worry about why this is; it may seem silly – but it works, so use it. Incidentally, use 99p rather than 95p – those extra 4p can mount up if your product sells in thousands.
- Range quotes: in a business where exact costing may be impossible, a quote may say that costs will be between £3,000 and £4,000, and that degree of uncertainty may be acceptable. A larger gap might not. Nor is going over the top limit; this can very often prevent reordering – 'They always go over their estimate.'
- Exact price for bespoke work: if you undertake work where what you propose is a unique method or approach for an individual client – like a computer system, printing or consultancy – then remember that it will not be seen as credible if it just happens to work out at an exact £10,000. Such a price will certainly encourage resistance. It will seem like the figure is either a calculation you have rounded up, or

that the service being offered is not, in fact, bespoke. And that may well devalue it when a tailored solution is wanted.

Make sure also that there is no confusion. Your price must be completely clear. If you charge for design, delivery or travel then say so and explain on what basis this is done. Money can easily be lost by queries about unclear information leading to part of the charge being dropped (and perhaps setting a precedent).

Justifying a high price is part practical – you do actually have to deliver value for money. It is also part confidence. Thus when someone asks, How much? rather than turning to jelly, you have to say, 'Just £XXX, and worth every pound, and it includes...' and emphasize the value. People want value. They want certainty. Neil Armstrong, the first man to walk on the moon, was asked what he had thought about during take-off. He is said to have recalled that there were hundreds of thousands of components in the machine below him and in every case NASA had given the contract to the lowest bidder. I doubt that knowing this did much for his confidence!

High price and high quality go hand in hand; you can use them both to build your business and secure profitability in tough times.

And another idea...

Price issues can easily produce paranoia. You go through what may be a long sales process with someone. They are interested, impressed and want to buy. Then you quote the price and their eyebrows shoot up – 'What? How much?'. You immediately feel vulnerable. You worry you will lose the sale in the next three seconds and, too often, your knee jerk reaction may be to concede. You offer a discount, you explain that the price quoted is not for orders like theirs; you get (save?) the order but profitability – and your best intentions – are diluted.

As a way of describing things that helps reduce price resistance, keep in mind the arithmetic signs, using them as a prompt to how you can describe your price in a way that maximizes value:

■ + Say you offer this plus that/you get this in addition to that (and do not assume that everything about your offering is obvious, there are many things here to describe).

■ − You can: reduce/lessen/eliminate or minimize this (whatever it is that needs reducing, for example operating costs or administrative hassle).

■ × This produces multiple opportunities or enhances service or produces more or greater satisfaction.

Finally, amortize the costs (ie spread them over a period: less than £100 a month or just under [say £96] sounds much more attractive than £1,150 for the year).

38

Outsource to survive

With the growing turmoil in the world economies, by which we mean the credit crunch, mortgage crises, food shortages and rising inflation, outsourcing can be the key to corporate survival in such a tough economic climate.

The drivers of this change are not so much technological, but changes in competition and how businesses operate and execute their strategies. If the internet is the means of change, the driver of change is the need to cut costs and improve core business processes in increasingly competitive global markets.

Action

If you want to gain competitive advantage for your business, you need to look outside the box at how outsourcing can give your organization both competitive advantage and capture market share. There are four different outsourcing drivers that you might consider:

1. *Globalization:* to remain competitive and to spur top-line growth, large companies enter foreign markets. Low-cost producers must now rely on outsourcing to exist in the global economy.

2. *Internet:* if it were needed, the global sourcing model is further evidence of the transition from an industrial economy to an information economy. The internet allows sophisticated remote monitoring in offshore locations (this is directly as a result of improved CRM technology).

3. *Core and non-core:* the third driver is the difference between core and non-core processes. Most non-core processes are suitable for outsourcing. Initially it was low-skilled jobs in manufacturing, call centres and computer coding that went abroad. Now it is human resources and knowledge skills – in the future it could be more high-skilled jobs such as accounting and engineering that will be outsourced.

4. *Offshoring outsourcing:* initially it was manufacturing products that went abroad, next will be backroom processing and services. This is due to the advent of reliable cheap global communications and the internet; also the abundance of skilled labour forces in many developing countries.

And another idea...

The main reason for outsourcing has always been cost savings. One of the biggest trends in outsourcing is offshoring. Countries such as India have a large supply of well-educated, English speaking candidates. By outsourcing functions such as call centres or accounting, operational expenses can be reduced by around half. Outsourcing's next tide is gathering momentum. Businesses that fail to find a way to swim with it will sink from lack of competitive advantage.

39

Mobility counts – being flexible to change

Change happens and there's not much you can do about it. Some people ignore it, others try to stop it. You could try insulating yourself from it, while others spend an enormous amount of energy fighting it.

Action

There are four phases through which people pass before they embrace change. These are

1. *Denial:* 'That's never going to work', 'We tried that already.' Do you recognize the 'ostriches' in your organization? They may have their heads in the sand, but change is not going to go away as a result of their not seeing it.

2. *Resistance:* Some people try to stick with the old ways of doing things. 'But it's always worked ok in the past.' The reality is, the sooner you get to grips with the new system, the better it is for results (and your blood pressure).

3. *Exploration:* Maybe the change doesn't have to be all bad. Is it possible that there are some advantages to the new way of

> working? If you look at the change with a more open mind, you may begin to find some good things that come from it.
>
> 4. *Acceptance:* Once you reach this stage, you may even find that the new system works better than you'd believed possible. You have by this time fully integrated the change into your own routine.

Watch out for the warning signs

There are a number of things that people may do while they cannot accept change:

■ use old methods of working when they should be playing by the new rules;

■ avoid taking on new assignments for fear that they might have to work in a different way;

■ try to slow things down to their own pace. Unfortunately change usually requires people to speed up, so they risk getting left further and further behind;

■ play the victim/martyr role. Unfortunately more flexible colleagues won't show them any sympathy;

■ try to control the uncontrollable. This is a bit like attempting to stop the tide from coming up the beach. Change is inevitable – they'll have to accept it. Instead of wasting energy resisting – they should go with the flow.

And another idea...

You may notice a number of colleagues whose behaviour is similar to that described above. Don't allow yourself to resist change. If you can show that you are willing to embrace it, people will quickly realize what an incredible asset you are to the organization. You're a survivor and your responsiveness to change will be your passport to future success.

40

Watching your figure(s) – cash flow and paying bills

Successful businesses are very meticulous when it comes to managing their cash flow. Even when they are facing tough times, their payroll continues to be met, invoices are settled and the organization can still manage (selectively) to move forward. How does this happen? By applying sound cash flow management skills.

Action

Pay late –companies will often ask for a net 30 day term when purchasing from a supplier. When someone is supposed to pay you, a cheque rarely turns up the day after you've sent the invoice. Part of this is due to accounting controls but the other part involves effectively managing cash flow.

Small businesses can easily take advantage of this same approach. Whenever you get a bill, whether it's for utilities, internet, credit card or office supplies, make a note of when payment is due. The payment is likely to be due between two and four weeks after you've received the invoice. When you pay a bill promptly you may get a warm satisfying glow, but you'll also have a hole in your bank account. The best advice is to pay the bill as close to the due date as possible without being late.

During this time you could transfer the money into a savings account to earn interest. Another way of taking advantage of delayed payment is to pay as many bills as you can with a credit card. If it's possible, control the statement date of your credit card to align with the due date of the bill. With a bit of luck and if you use the grace period offered by both your creditor and your credit card company, you could delay writing the cheque for 45–60 days after the service has been invoiced and provided.

You need to use that time frame to earn interest on your money and collect in some additional payments owed to you in order to build up your cash flow.

It takes time to organize, but once you've got the hang of it, it makes total sense.

And another idea...

If you intend to get a real grip on what state the organization's finances are in, there are three steps that you need to take: review, monitor and act. First you need to review your financial position every six months. Then you must monitor on a monthly basis exactly where the money goes. That includes doing a bank reconciliation to see that there aren't any errors. Banks do make mistakes sometimes. Finally based on a study of that expenditure, you need to act to ensure that you either make savings or economies to ease cash flow, or you work with your money (if you have a surplus) so that it earns interest while it is sitting in the bank.

41

Quick change promotion

The fleeting attention spans of people in the modern age are legionary. Sound bites have replaced anything of any length and it is a principle that applies firmly to promotion of many sorts. Attitudes to that are routinely fleeting too, and are coupled with an 'I've seen it all before' outlook. Thus any promotion you may do in tough times, and Chapter 21 suggests that much must continue, must be both focused and designed to get attention. Now let us be clear here, one of the things that makes (good) advertising effective is repetition. Major companies do not repeat their advertising nightly on television or put their posters on every street corner without purpose; seeing things again and again gets the message home.

But there are some kinds of promotion where this principle is not so valid. Consider a shop. It may be well-located and have the same people walking by every day, say on their way to work. They look at the window display. As they go past the next day they look again. Repeated looking reinforces whatever message is presented there; but this effect is one of diminishing returns. All too soon they are not really looking any more, certainly not if a glance tells them that they have seen it all before. Once the window is changed, in whole or part, then the effect re-starts, and the chances of someone being prompted to enter the shop are increased.

How quickly must things change? For many shops it might be sensible to do so weekly, and, yes, it is a chore (albeit not a very expensive one) but it is worthwhile. In one bookshop I know (PF) they have a number of display stands on wheels. Every day they turn them ninety degrees so that what faces the front of the shop is different. That's very easy to do and yes, they say it makes a measurable difference to sales.

The same is true of something like a website. If you sell that way, even to a small degree, have a look at one of your favourites. Certainly this is true of Amazon if we stick with books for the moment. Every time you log on there is something new to see: new displays, new recommendations, new products and more. Why? For precisely the reasons just explained: they are increasing the chance of prompting new business, the purchase of something other than what someone logged on for.

Action

In order to increase effectiveness in tough times this is an area that can have an immediate effect. Check what goes on in your business. Do you have a shop window, a reception area, a showroom, leaflets, newsletter or a website? Any of these can do more for you if more people find them new and different more of the time.

And another idea...

If you find something like a window display or newsletter difficult to refresh on so regular a basis there are several things you can do:

■ Do some research; see what others are doing and whether any ideas they have could work for you. Look at both competitive and non-competitive areas and consider asking others how things are working.

- Collaborate. Window displays are a good example of this; you will often see something like a deck chair in the travel agent's window that is borrowed from (or swapped with) another retailer.
- In addition, check with your suppliers: they may have ways to help you beef up this sort of promotion and to help you keep ringing the changes, both in terms of ideas and resources.

Whatever you do, make sure that you never delude yourself that it does the job for ever. If you want to change the market, then you may have to change something first (and continue doing so).

42

Increasing price (without increasing price)

The question of overall pricing policy is highlighted in Chapter 37; here are different pricing considerations that deserve separate comment. You set your price at say (let's just pick a simple currency-free figure) 100. You know your margins and want to see if you can get more from all or some of your sales. How can you do this?

Well, consider how price appears. What about the price for petrol? Okay you may think it's high and too much of it is tax, but you will notice something else as well – it is not sold at the same price per litre in every outlet. Some people are making more money from it than others, despite some of the shopping around that such practice may prompt.

Action

It is worth a careful review of how you can maximize price. Even a marginal difference, repeated many times, can add up and help bridge financial gaps with which you may be struggling. Your price is 100, but can it be a little more in some places? For example, your own website might sell at a (slightly) raised price, perhaps coupled with giving more – express delivery perhaps, or a discount off future purchases (something designed to influence future sales and customer loyalty). Direct sales also means there is no necessity to give a discount to a middleman, so profitability is better anyway.

A variety of tactics are possible, though ahead of listing some examples it should perhaps be noted that not all of them go unobserved by customers. You may want to balance the financial effects with others. For example:

- Pack size: a number of food companies have been criticized for reducing the size of their product – like a chocolate bar – while retaining the same price. This is effectively a price increase.
- Extras: with some products the number of elements that need to be paid for in addition to the basic price is lengthy; motor cars are a good example. Even one element added beyond the basic price is effectively a price increase.
- Timescale: timing can leave customers at a disadvantage and have a company increasing its profits, as with for example a savings account rapidly falling in the tables as new accounts are introduced.
- De luxe: research shows that when a company offers two similar products, one the 'Rolls Royce' version of the other at a premium price, the majority of customers chooses the higher priced. This is usually configured so that it is also the most profitable; the extra features do not cost as much as the price difference.
- Link to other factors: many mobile phones are cheap or free, the profit comes from the calls. At the other end of the scale, the cost of industrial equipment may be linked in a

similar way to servicing and spare parts. Such links are possible with many products.

▓ Trade discount: while the price of a book, say, may be the same in a chain store and an independent book shop, they will likely have been given different discounts (the chain store will have obtained a greater discount); different outlets selling the same products therefore can produce different profits.

As has been said, such tactics must be used with care, but some valid increase in profitability is usually possible through reviewing such factors.

And another idea...

Discounts can be given on a variety of bases (like the large and small retailer above), but in tough times you need to see that, wherever possible, you gain something from the process. Quantity discounts is perhaps the prime example; the unit price is less, but only when more are bought; it is a deal that can suit both parties. Alternatively, discounts may be linked to other advantages such as a discount for a cash payment or the purchase of another (perhaps related) product.

43

Leave no stone unturned to stimulate sales

For the small business even quite small marketing expenditure may be daunting. Yet something must be done. Even the most excellent shop cannot regard opening the door at 9 am as promotion, and we treasure the apocryphal story of the business that opened with the proprietor saying that 'With such an excellent product, no promotion is necessary'; they prevailed in this belief right up to the time they had to erect a 'For Sale' sign outside their premises. Something must be done, but what doesn't incur major expense?

Action

The action here is twofold. First, consider the range of things that you might do – they must suit your business, so the possibilities are endless. 'Consider' needs defining: you may need to do some research, read some books, observe what others do and more but, however it is done, you need to assemble a list of low-cost promotional methods and select some as priorities to try.

Second, you need to set yourself some targets. The trick here is to have something being done on a (very) regular basis. One such methodology may be as simple as a letter sent every day or week; whatever is involved make sure you create a systematic way of ensuring that it happens and happens regularly. Just a letter every day is well over 200 a year (ignoring weekends, etc.) and conditions may then have improved. But if even 10 per cent respond, you might have 20 or more new customers – and, of course, the numbers responding and the sales revenue they produce could be much higher.

All sorts of simple methods can be found, for example:

- send a postcard (used effectively in the travel trade);
- send Christmas or birthday cards to customers – and include some (promotional) news;
- send customers copies of other things you do, for example a press release, or a resulting mention in a newspaper or magazine;
- send reminders, such as when a car is due a service;
- put messages into special formats, for instance on sheets punched to fit a Filofax;
- issue notices to go on your customers' notice boards, in the way that a travel agent handling executive travel might make offers to staff for their holidays;
- put your message (or part of it) on a Post-it note;
- circulate testimonials (linked to a promotional message);
- provide a sticker for their telephone to remind them of your order line.

Make and extend your own list; it can pay dividends. Monitor the results too and extend the use of those methods that prove most successful.

And another idea...

Do not dismiss things as too simple. This book started life as a note to the publisher that said:

Are you an optimist or a pessimist? Can you turn a book round fast? How about a title on surviving a recession?

That's not even two lines, yet sending it to just two publishers created a project and if you bought this copy (rather than, say, borrowing it) then the royalty from that sale is helping us through difficult times! If so, thank you. So do not reject low cost ideas – there are many that can be useful. Have a go and keep doing so in simple ways. Some initiatives may fall on stony ground, but some will pay off.

44

Being memorable

It's always good if people remember you. Unless of course you behave so badly or look so peculiar they can't forget you. One way to make a positive impact on people is by being outstanding. If you can do this, you could find work a little easier when going through a rough patch.

Action

Face-to-face dealings

When it comes to dealing with people on a face-to-face basis, there are a few simple things it is worth remembering. None of this is 'rocket science', but do you make the effort to do it when times are hard?

1. Speak to people courteously.
2. Smile rather than frown.
3. Remember to address them by name.
4. Be helpful and friendly.
5. Show interest and be considerate to their feelings.
6. Be a good listener rather than a talker.
7. Be enthusiastic.

Written communication

Now, how interesting is this seminar invitation:

We are arranging a seminar at our offices on 26 August at 5.30pm for the purpose of explaining what the changes to the tax depreciation policy announced by the Government recently will mean for our major customers.

Compared to this:

Good news. You may have less tax to pay next year. The Government's recent announcement on depreciation will help most companies like yours, some considerably, others only slightly. Would you like to hear more? If so come to our free seminar on...

One rule: write not so that you can be understood, but so that you cannot be misunderstood. If there is ambiguity, the written word will always be construed negatively.

And another idea...

Remember that sometimes you only have a few seconds to communicate an idea or message to someone. This could be when being interviewed, or quoted in an article. Your 'lift pitch' should be clear and concise. As an example, here are some memorable lines. Can you remember who spoke these words?

'I shall never tell a lie.'

'Come up and see me sometime.'

'Friends, Romans, Countrymen, lend me your ears.'

'I'm a pretty honest kind of guy.'

'Ich bin ein Berliner.'

'One small step for man, a giant leap for mankind.'

New ways of looking at things

When business is difficult it might help to do some 'blue sky' thinking. Some immutable laws of marketing:

Action

1. It is better to be first than it is to be better. For example, Charles Lindbergh was the first to fly across the Atlantic; Bert Hinkler was the better pilot, flew faster and used less fuel, but, importantly, wasn't first.

2. If you can't be first in a category, set up a new category you can be first in. Amelia Earhart was only the third person to fly solo across the Atlantic, but was the first woman pilot to do so.

3. The most powerful concept in marketing is owning a word in the prospect's mind: safety – Volvo; driving – BMW; engineering – Mercedes; technology – Audi.

4. In the long run, every market becomes a two-horse race: Tesco/Wal-Mart; Ford/General Motors; Coke/Pepsi.

5. Two companies cannot own the same word in the prospect's mind: fast belongs to MacDonald's, not Burger King – they have 'flame-grilled'.

And another idea…

Without adequate funding, an idea will not get off the ground. Are you a Bert Hinkler (a me-too)? Could you lead the market in something? What's your word?

46

Big stick or kid gloves (the right approach to dealing with difficult staff)

If only people worked harmoniously all the time. Even when the economy is healthy this is rarely the case. When the business climate is rather stormy, people can often behave badly, which does nothing to help those running the organizations.

Action

Some tips for dealing with tricky situations:

1. If someone trips up once or twice, perhaps a gentle reminder is all that's required. If it happens on a regular basis, morale plummets and the management must act.

2. Everyone in the workplace is entitled to be treated with dignity and respect. Bullying, harassment and discrimina-

tion should not be tolerated. Companies should have policies and procedures for dealing with grievance and disciplinary matters. Check that yours is in place and up to date with regard to current employment law.

3. If you need to take action, you must be clear about what steps are involved. You don't want to end up in front of an employment tribunal.

4. Discipline should not be confused with punishment. Discipline is positive; punishing someone is to do with exacting a penalty. Disciplining an employee can be an informal or formal procedure, depending on the severity of the problem.

5. Set a good example by dealing with an issue fast. Maintain fair procedures, set standards of behaviour by means of an organisational policy (issued to all staff) via the company handbook. There is a clear distinction between issues related to performance and misconduct. Be sure you identify the problem.

And another idea...

Because employment law is so complicated, be sure to consult your human resources professional or company lawyer before taking any action. There are some great resources to be found on the ACAS website, including the ACAS code of practice (www.acas.org.uk). Should matters come to a head, remember to keep copies of everything to do with the disciplinary procedure.

47

Top ten ideas for keeping afloat on rough waters

Here are ten action points for success – when the going gets rough:

1. Have an ambitious vision – but be realistic.
2. Convert those you perceive as enemies into friends.
3. Always employ the best possible people, across a variety of skills sets.
4. Hire the best consultants you can afford (don't tolerate incompetence).
5. Choose business associates you would happily take home to meet your family.
6. People make things work, not spreadsheets.
7. Even with different types of organizations, there aren't that many differences.
8. Government initiatives always follow rather than lead the curve.
9. Plan, plan, plan and then have a fall-back plan.
10. Don't go past your sell-by date. Be prepared to take a risk.

And another idea...

Choosing the wrong managing director is the fastest way to fail.

48

Wow! – the power of service excellence

In tough times you need every order and every customer possible. It is a truism that it is easier to sell something more to existing customers than find new ones. And nothing is more likely to prompt repeat orders than good, and preferably excellent, service. So it follows that you need to work hard at ensuring this is so.

Action

The action here is twofold:

- First, make sure that your customer handling activities and system are as they should be and are guided by customers rather than internal convenience and bureaucracy. What this involves will vary depending on the nature of your organization, but time spent here is worthwhile.

- Second, look too at your complaint handling procedures. If service is good you won't get too many, but if/when you do, regard them as an opportunity – if they can be sorted efficiently then the end result can be that customers are actually more likely to do business with you again than if nothing untoward had happened (though don't encourage complaints for that reason!).

And another idea...

An area that stands some review is that of automated telephone systems. By this I mean the ones that quote you options – press one – play you horrid music and spew out trite little phrases like 'Calls may be recorded to help us provide excellent service', when just getting through to them is the very reverse of excellent service. One of us (PF) recently spent long minutes listening to options and pressing buttons only to be told, 'We're currently closed.' Tell us that at once! This sort of thing has become part of life, the butt of jokes, and yet affects choice very directly. How many people opt out part way through such a labyrinth, and go elsewhere so that business is lost by whoever was in fact their first choice? It bears thinking about.

Improved ratios/ increased sales

Sales, in terms of overall sales technique, has already been mentioned (see Chapter 32) and everything that can be done to improve strike rate here should be done. This section addresses an area that often gets overlooked when sales are flowing in reasonably well – that of improving strike rate through whatever chain of stages leads to an order in a particular business. Analysis can improve sales results in a number of different ways and free up time that can then be used to approach additional prospects.

Action

The first stage is to think through what typically goes on. Some business, for example past customers happy to reorder and doing so without preamble, circumvents the longest chain here and need concern you less.

Each list of such a chain is a little different in different organizations, but by way of example consider the following:

- Promotional activity leads the way.

- Some people seeing this contact the company for more information.

- Some of those receiving more information in whatever way (from telephone contact, brochures or website) ask to see someone.

- A sales person has a meeting with them (it could be more than one).

- Some people will want a formal quotation or proposal (and there could be other stages such as a presentation, demonstration or sample depending on the nature of the product or service).

- While some orders may come now (or earlier), other prospects need following up – by phone, email, in person or whatever is appropriate.

- Finally, you can log the number of firm orders that come through the 'system'.

It should be noted here that by its nature this process is wasteful. If prospects drop out at a late stage (at worst because they feel that something has been done inadequately) then the time and cost it took to get them that far is gone for ever, and a similar investment of time and effort needs to be made to get another prospect through. In tough times this kind of wastage is something very much to be avoided.

It does not matter whether your list of stages is longer or shorter than the example above, the second action is then the same in principle. You need to put some numbers to the conversion rate. Let's say, for instance, that only 10 per cent of people receiving details move on to do more, or that half the people sales people meet with agree to a formal proposal being submitted, or that half the people getting proposals actually commit to an order. The question then is, can these conversions be improved?

If, again just as an example, the ratio of proposal documents to orders seems poor, perhaps a different type of proposal (or just a better written one) might change things. Often the overall ratio is high: we will resist putting numbers to it as businesses differ too much, but many prospects must go in at one end for each single firm order resulting.

There is often plenty of scope for action and improvement in this situation and taking it has two additional advantages. First, it improves differentiation throughout the sales process. If you can win enough sales from (less aware) competitors it may make up for a shrunken market. Second, the changes indicated are often not high in time or cost to achieve, which is just what you want in tough times.

And another idea...

Action in this area, and perhaps others too of course, is something that can be shared around. If there is a sales team, getting each member to do some investigation and think about possible changes in discrete areas of the process is more manageable than one person struggling to review and change everything. Provided everything is pulled together and any changes well communicated (something that may involve formal changes to policy and practice), all this can result in significant and rapid change.

50

Maximizing web business

Technology has a way of creeping up on you. One day the internet is an uncertain prediction, now we are all learning to surf and references to e-commerce are all around. You may have bought this book by contacting a website (the publisher, Kogan Page, has one: www.koganpage.com), and many businesses of all sorts, even small ones, have their own website. Indeed to create a simple website is now a classic low-cost option.

Leaving the technology aside (as it is beyond our brief), a website is no more than a new option in the promotional mix and needs to be considered accordingly. Setting up a website can be time-consuming and expensive; so too can maintaining it and keeping it up to date. But it compares favourably with many other sorts of marketing option, and is something that can be got under way quickly. Whether you are starting from scratch or if your website is simple, perhaps out of date and due an overhaul, this is something to address as soon as tough times appear on the horizon. Indeed a (good) website provides a separate, perhaps additional, way of doing business. Whatever might be done to ensure this is or will be working effectively needs thinking through; the action starts with a basic first question that is very obvious and straightforward.

Action

That first question is, what objectives do you have for your website?

There may be several, but they should all be specific. It is important to know whether the cost of setting this up is delivering what was intended; important, not least, to know how a site is developed. Perhaps the site is in part a source of reference. You want people to consult it to obtain information (and be impressed by it at the same time). This may save time and effort otherwise expended in other ways. Perhaps you intend that it plays a more integral part in the selling process, and you want to measure its effectiveness in terms of counting the number of new contacts it produces and, in turn, how many of those are turned into actual revenue-producing customers. So, if you already have a website check whether you have good feedback on its use and know the specific results it brings you (for example, counting new contacts or money coming from new customers). Similarly, if you are in the process of setting up a site ensure consideration of this is an inherent part of the process.

In addition, you may have products you want people to order and pay for through direct contact with the site. A consultant might offer a survey of some sort, primarily to put an example of their expertise and style in the hands of prospective clients (though it might be a source of revenue also). In this case not only must the ordering system work well, and this means it must be quick and easier for whoever is doing the ordering, but the follow-up must be good too. Any initial good impression given will quickly evaporate if whatever is ordered takes forever to arrive or needs several chasers. One hazard to good service is to demand too much information as an order is placed. Of course, this kind of contact represents an opportunity to create a useful database; but turning ordering into the Spanish Inquisition will hardly endear you to people.

Whatever objectives are decided upon, there are then three distinct tasks. They are to:

- attract people to the site: just having the site set up does not mean people will log onto it in droves, much less that the people you want to do so will act in this way. Other aspects of promotion must draw attention to it and this may vary from simply having the website address on your letterhead to incorporating mention (and perhaps demonstration) of it into customer events;
- impress people when they see it: both with its content and its presentation. This means keeping a close eye on customers' views and the practicalities as it is set up. For example, all sorts of impressive graphics and pictures are possible and can look creative and may well impress. Certainly you will need some. But such devices take a long time to download, and if that is what you are encouraging people to do they may find this tedious, especially if the graphics seem more like window dressing than something that enhances the content in a useful way;
- encourage repeat use: this may or may not be one of the objectives. If it is then efforts have to be made to encourage re-contacting and this too may involve an overlap with other forms of communication.

Beyond this you also need to consider carefully:

- what the content should be (this is an ongoing job, not a one-off);
- how contacting the website can prompt a dialogue;
- how topical it should be (this affects how regularly it needs revision);
- its convenience and accessibility (does it have a suitable navigation mechanism?);
- whether it will look consistent (and not as if it has been put together by committee);
- the protection it needs (is anything confidential, is it vulnerable to hackers, etc).

Overall, it will need the same planning, co-ordination and careful execution as any other form of marketing communication. In addition, it is likely to necessitate active, ongoing co-operation from numbers of people around the organization who will provide and update information. Given how difficult it can be to get even a small group of people to agree on, say, one page of copy for a new brochure, this may present quite a challenge. Clearly responsibility for the site and what it contains must be unequivocally laid at someone's door, together with the appropriate authority to see it through.

In addition, someone needs to have the knowledge that is necessary from a technical standpoint. This may be internal or external, but it needs to be linked to an understanding of marketing and/or the ability to accept a clear brief. This is not a case of applying all the available technology, building in every bell and whistle simply because it is possible. Practical solutions are necessary to meet clear objectives.

If a site is to be not just useful, but an effective part of a marketing mix tailored to tough times, then sufficient time and effort must be put in to get it right. And the ongoing job of maintaining it must be borne in mind from the beginning. Log on. Have a look. And get thinking about how it might work better.

And another idea...

An interesting and practical development is the availability of standard, cost effective software packages that can work as an integral part of a website and monitor how it is used. In fact, there are now such add-ons better described as research tools. One such, ONQUEST, allows regular research and formal monthly analysis about exactly who is using a website, their precise characteristics, and how and why they are in touch with the site. It allows the way the system works to be simply tailored to the needs and intentions of an individual organization. The intention is specifically to obtain information that will make the website a more accurate and effective marketing tool. Such software can be added to a website quickly and easily and is almost guaranteed to make your marketing targeting more effective.

Similarly, other technological possibilities come along in increasing profusion. For example, it is possible for someone logged on to a website to trigger a phone call from a supplier. Thus you can organize to be able to talk to a potential customer as they look at your site, or afterwards if that is more convenient to them. Service enhancements such as this can also pay dividends in tough market conditions when customers may need only a nudge to select one supplier rather than another.

This whole area changes and develops as you watch. There are opportunities not to be missed but, as this short section makes clear, it needs to be approached in the right way or effort can be dissipated without real advantage.

51

New prospects – focusing to create the best potential

Apart from the quality of face-to-face selling techniques (certainly an area of major influence), for those doing the selling there are only three key matters that influence sales results. They are:

- who you see – which particular prospects and customers you spend time with;
- how many you see – selling is very much a matter of productivity; in general terms if you see more people then, all other things being equal, you will sell more;
- how often you see them – the question of frequency of contact with people needing regular visits is vital (too little and there is no continuity or relationship developed, too much and over-calling reduces productivity and the number of new people you can see).

Before you even consider which people you will see, you have to be able to take action that will result in a meeting.

Seeing the right people

Two comments are relevant under this heading:

- In some businesses the potential market is way beyond what the individual can contact. For example, if you sell office equipment, photocopiers or binding machines, then even limiting the potential market to offices (and some people have offices at home), the market is huge.
- Which people do you attempt to see? The largest companies? The nearest? Those ones in a particular industry? And what kind of person do you see? Who uses the equipment, who has the budget, who makes the purchase decision? This might be the managing director of some organizations and a secretary in others. And, of course, they will not all need it and, even if they do, that need may already have been satisfied – perhaps your main competitor sold them a machine yesterday. Superficially they may all seem like prospects. Not all acorns grow into giant oak trees; most are eaten by the pigs. Even those that register an enquiry are not equal prospects either.

So you must set priorities. Sales people who allow their time to be wasted on those who exhibit no real potential, the 'no-hopers', perhaps because they are in some way easy to access, will never do as well as those who accept that priorities must be set and then do so systematically. In tough times anything but a clear focus will risk sales being less than they might.

Trust your own experience, and never ignore the evidence of the past. Ask yourself who has purchased previously, and why. Think through the logic of contacting one person rather than others and concentrate your activities and your efforts for example, on those which analysis shows are the best prospects. If you sell in certain areas, such as consumer products to retail outlets, this problem may hardly exist as the outlets are comparatively few in number and contact is established with them all. The incidence of new ones that need assessing in terms of potential is less. For others it is key, and their success is in direct proportion to the time and sensible thought put into deciding who to see and who not to see; at least not yet. Who you decide to see is perhaps the first decision that influences whether a sale is likely to result; so choose carefully.

Who is the buyer?

This may at first sight seem a stupid question. At one level you need to identify the person who buys: QED. However, the buyer is often, particularly in industrial selling, more than one person, or at least more than one plays a part in the buying process. It is useful to categorize the different roles that may be involved. An example illustrates the principle. For example, someone sells computers; think of a primarily wordprocessing use for them:

- *The user:* assume this is a typist or secretary who will have opinions about what they want and of any suggested option. Today most executives may well input material themselves, and so will be users too.
- *Advisors:* these people act as advisors to someone who will make the decision, perhaps the administration director, if the whole company is to use common equipment. The accountant may well be an advisor also, at least on cost, contracts and servicing.

And if the company has a purchasing department someone there may be the buyer who is actually influenced by all those others already mentioned and who has, in addition, a measure of authority, large or small themselves.

- *Decision makers:* when the final recommendation, or short list, is in, it may be the managing director who is the decision maker. Having said all that, the person who rings up in the first instance and asks for a brochure may be someone quite different, such as the accountant's assistant.

Actually, given the multiple tasks computers are used for, this might be more complicated. You must never assume that whoever initiates contact, or responds to your overtures to see them is, by definition, the ultimate decision maker. You need to know what role they actually play, who else is involved and how the ultimate decision will be made. This may only emerge as the contact is progressed, and the information about how it all works may need to be actively unearthed by active, but careful, questioning.

To add a small complication, there is another category that is worth attention and which plays a part in all this. They are usually called the gatekeepers.

Such people prohibit or allow access to others in the decision making array. This might imply a secretary or assistant, but might also be someone more senior; for example an architect might allow (or not) access to the client, the ultimate decision maker about a building project. Recognize them and nurture them; they can be an invaluable boost to your chances of selling successfully.

Action

Finding the best prospects

The balance of managing existing customers and yet constantly finding sufficient new ones to grow and develop the business is crucial in selling many kinds of product and service. Yet it is all too often something that is found difficult, distasteful and neglected; one feels there is a clear link here between these factors. It is precisely because prospecting is inclined to be difficult to fit in amongst other work priorities, and do justice to, that it must be approached systematically and made a priority when every sale matters.

Make prospecting a regular activity

There can be hardly a sales person who does not find 'cold calling' less attractive than calling on existing customers. This is not surprising. It is unlikely to be easy, the strike rate is likely to be lower and, by definition, the rejection rate will be higher. Yet many businesses need the lifeblood of a constant supply of new prospects at least to some extent. If you need a regular supply of potential new customers, then you must recognize that the activity to produce them must itself be carried out regularly. It is a common fault of many sales people that they neglect or put off action in this area, allowing an insufficient number of prospects to become a major problem.

If new contacts are the lifeblood of your business, make your first rule of prospecting: do it, and do it systematically and regularly.

And another idea...

Set time aside every week, link prospecting to regular activities and do not let other short-term pressures give you the excuse to neglect it. If it is important, then prospecting must have its own targets. Ensure it is done regularly and that the returns you get from it – new people to add to those you sell to – will help you achieve the results you want even in less than ideal market conditions.

52

It's a matter of attitude

You may find it difficult to keep a positive outlook when you are swimming against the tide. But if you are prone to making negative statements, try to turn them into positive ones instead. (For example – 'I can't stop eating' becomes 'I only eat when I need to, and then I always eat healthy food.')

Action

1. Train your brain to accept only the messages you want to accept. Don't allow it to absorb negative information.

2. When faced with a problem, look for a solution, not a reason to give up.

3. Remember – you only fail when you quit.

4. The central nervous system cannot tell the difference between a real and an imagined event. If you can convince your subconscious of what you want you will instinctively start taking the actions that will make it happen for you.

5. Problems that you can overcome become positive experiences. Consider what you can learn from things that have turned out differently to your original expectations.

And another idea...

Wise words to bear in mind:

Whether you think you can, or whether you think you can't – either way you're right.

(Henry Ford)

Afterword

There is little more to say as we intend that the chapters of this book speak for themselves both in terms of individual topics and the overall imperative to take action rather than waiting for things to get back to normal.

The principle of action based on review and consideration has been commended throughout the piece. In addition it is perhaps fitting to end on an optimistic note. Perhaps the following classic tale makes a useful point.

The tale, from medieval times, is about a servant in the King's household who is condemned to life imprisonment for some small misdemeanour. Languishing in his cell, a thought struck him and he sent a message to the King promising that, if he were released, he would work day and night and, within a year, he would teach the King's favourite horse to talk.

This amused the King, and he ordered the servant to be released to work in the royal stables. The servant's friends were at once pleased to see him released, yet frightened for him too; after all, horses do not talk, however much training they get. 'What will you do?', they all asked. 'So much can happen in a year', he replied. 'I may die, the King may die, or – who knows – the horse may talk!'

Who knows indeed; and we might well hope that by the time the year was up he had thought of another ruse.

This attitude of purposeful optimism is to be commended. However tough times may affect you, they will have less negative effect if you try to minimize that effect. You may not get things 'back to normal', but thorough and systematic action can see you emerge in better shape than might appear possible at the start.

The ideas here can help, can start some thinking in train or prompt you to add additional tactics which will also help. Many things you do can ease the pain just a little, either directly or indirectly in the way something like good delegation frees a manager from routine and let's them spend more time creatively seeking solutions. Consult too – good ideas don't care who has them – everyone may have something to contribute (so maybe this book should be passed around to allow it to stimulate different people in different ways).

One thing is sure, there is nothing worse than to find yourself analysing the aftermath of a tough period and doing so with a comment that begins with the words 'If only …'.